MW00831794

The
EXECUTIVE
HORSE

21st Century Leadership Lessons from Horses

Evelyn McKelvie

Printed in Canada by Equine Coach Publishing

McKelvie, Evelyn

The Executive Horse: 21st Century Leadership Lessons from Horses

Acknowledgements

This book is dedicated to all horses who have so selflessly given us their cooperation, trust, and patience, to those horses I have met with my deepest gratitude for being so forgiving and generous in nature, and I especially dedicate this book to Easter's Hurricane, AKA 'Harold', who taught me so much about horses, about myself, and about unconditional love.

I also wish to thank the many people who helped me complete this major undertaking, especially Sophie Bartek, Rosemary Smyth, Jill Lambert, Chris Irwin, Duncan Holmes, Julie Salisbury, and the Penning Divas.

And lastly I thank my family and friends who have supported me or tolerated me for all these years in my crazy passion for horses.

Testimonials

"I went into a day with Evelyn McKelvie as coach with a big huh? But from nervous, skeptical beginnings, Evelyn paired me with a teacher who offered pure magic. Cricket was my partner, and what happened between us lingered as a memorable lesson for life—how we might relate to those around us in whatever we do. The experience was unforgettable.

We didn't ride our horses that day. Just 'whispered' with them, and savored their wisdom. Evelyn's book tells the story, and when you're ready, you can join her for a very different, very rewarding ride. You'll want to do it again."

Duncan Holmes, Journalist (Canadian Press, Vancouver Sun), Vice-President Communications, Keg Restaurants, Special Lifetime Achievement Award winner, and contributor for publications such as Quench magazine.

"With great pleasure and deep appreciation, I truly savoured each sentence of The Executive Horse. *A delightful "page turner", Evelyn McKelvie's beautifully written odyssey flows seamlessly with profound insights for personal and professional change.*

"A critically needed paradigm shift in thinking for the vulnerable times we live, The Executive Horse *is a must read for those of us with the courage and compassion to lead as Shepherds of Emotional Intelligence."*

Chris Irwin is a widely respected, internationally renowned, equine trainer, clinician, author, and speaker, and devotes much of his time to his Equine Assisted Personal Development program.

Dedication

To Amos

Contents

Contents

Preface

This book is intended for business leaders, change agents, coaches and trainers, and for anyone who has a passion for learning and self-actualization or is responsible for organizational culture, workplace wellness, and performance development. This book is for those who believe that people can change – that we can change ourselves and the world we live in, that we can alter the trajectory of seemingly endless wars, extreme economic disparity, violence, and relentless climate change, and by using the higher gifts of the human spirit, we can rise above the limits of our history and move closer to a Utopian ideal.

I came to this work of equine facilitated executive coaching via a circuitous path. My career has been non-traditional, starting in the field of the performing arts, progressing through leadership roles in private and public education - both teaching and administrative - ultimately leading to a management career in Information Technology. Along the winding road I have always been inspired to pursue new avenues of learning and to find ways to help people achieve and develop to their maximum potential.

In 1998 I made a life changing discovery that set me on a path to another new career – a career that I didn't think existed at the time - becoming a Certified Executive Coach and horse trainer. Combining these two seemingly disparate career paths has become a life passion and enabled the perfect channel for consolidating my total life experience with a mission to serve others.

The Executive Horse is about transformational change through equine facilitated executive coaching. It is about a different way of looking at leadership - one that fits into the kinds of organizations that are being built today by Gen Xers and millennials. It is about cross-cultural leadership. It is about a kind of open heart, open mind, transparent way of being in the workplace, and everywhere else we find ourselves.

In this book I will describe how I became fascinated by the power of the horse, offer insight into how and why the relationship with horses is so powerfully transformative for people, and how, in the 21st century, horses are still working side by side with us to help humans evolve and make our world a better place. I will also describe some of the theoretical models that are a basis for the work I do, and the way I do it.

You likely have never heard of equine-assisted learning, healing, or coaching, but it is a growing field demonstrating effectively a method of engaging people and creating powerful learning opportunities. In order to absorb, change, and tackle the difficult issues that can get in the way of personal and organizational effectiveness, transformational change is required at a speed not normally seen in humans. And yet cases of rapid personal and systemic transformation do occur and put the lie to the notion that nothing ever changes.

I have made the horse an integral part of this mode of coaching for a number of reasons. Horses are highly social animals. Perhaps more than humans, their survival depends on their having, and fitting into, a herd. Horses model a way of being that is without judgment and yet very grounded in emotion and the present. Horses are what I call EMF (electro-magnetic field) detectors. The survival strategy of the horse is largely based on their ability to detect from afar, the emotional state and intention of other beings in their field of view, and beyond. They need to know who goes there - friend or foe. Lacking opposable thumbs and armed only with teeth and hammer-like hooves, their primary method of avoiding becoming lunch is to flee. As prey animals their viability is dependent on knowing if the predators around them are looking for lunch or have already eaten. Horses form strong emotional bonds with herd mates, and are prepared to accept non-equines into the herd, similar to the way dogs will accept humans as part of the pack. They need to know if those who are trying to join the herd are an asset to the team. If not, they are likely to expel you as a threat.

These characteristics make horses ideally suited to coaching people who seek to change themselves, their lives, and their organizations or herds. It is these same-yet-strangely-different characteristics of the horse that engage us so powerfully and create the perfect opportunities for the Aha! moments that precede having our minds opened and changed. We can relate to them socially and emotionally and yet be surprised and perplexed by their responses to simple gestures and instincts. Their fragile power has fascinated us for thousands of years and earned them a special place in our non-human family relationships.

Can People Change? Can Organizations Learn?

This question is at the root of much investment in organizations today; doing more with less and fewer people means the ones you hire and keep have to be more productive than ever before. When organizations must reorganize to stay competitive and profitable, then people must change or leave. The strategic arc of our evolution proves we homo-sapiens are wired to learn and adapt, a characteristic that has led to our success as a species for tens of thousands of years. Nevertheless it appears that tactically, we as individuals are resistant to change and require compelling motivation to activate our willingness to do things differently.

Interestingly, we haven't made the same breakthroughs in understanding and changing our behaviour that we have made in technology. Despite the massive amount of data and knowledge we have collected in the last two thousand years or so, we have not outrun our neurophysiology. We have evolved sophisticated political systems, legal and moral codes of conduct, methods of creating international treaties and complex social systems but these are fragile as we can see in many areas of the world.

It is now a well-accepted idea that we humans will only thrive in the 21st century if we are prepared to deal with change as it comes at us faster and faster. In order to meet the future we have to be lifelong learners, creative, flexible and adaptive. Learning is important, not just for peoples' continued growth and development, but for the health and prosperity of the organizations in which we work, and for the sustainability of the world in which we live. Organizations are not learning organizations if individuals are not motivated to continuously learn, or if the organization does not support a culture of learning. It is now considered an axiom that performance, people, and profit are parts of a three-legged triangle. The parts are interdependent, one part affecting and being affected by the others.

Simply turning over staff with reorgs is damaging to organizations. The institutional knowledge loss and the effect on organizational culture and morale, although hard to measure, can be devastating to the bottom line. Performance Management is the Big Idea that hopes to solve that problem. However companies seem to be chronically unhappy with Performance Management tools and processes. For the effort expended, are they achieving better performance? If not, then how do we manage people smartly to produce better results?

A fundamental assumption of mine and a basis for the work that I do is that - yes! – people can and do change. In order to foster the right conditions for healthy change we need to accommodate the innate design of the human brain and the way we lead people.

Organizational Culture-
the Driver of Resistance or Revolution

Organizational culture is the wheelhouse of the learning organization. Organizational culture is a whole that is greater than the sum of the individual parts; i.e. the culture of an organization is the outcome of the shared beliefs, values, assumptions, and expectations of the members of the organization. Culture is also very much about the shared emotional affect of the organization - the felt sense of how individuals are when they are at work, how they perceive what others feel, the quality of their relationships, and the meaning they make of this ephemeral environmental 'soup'.

When the emotional affect of an organization is impaired by stress resulting from layoffs, a culture of bullying, micromanagement, a mindset of lack, or plain old inadequate leadership, the organization will manifest dysfunctions in its performance, people, and its profit.

Learning for people and organizations does not really occur under stress. Instead, neuroscientific research about learning has revealed the negative impact of stress and anxiety and the qualitative improvement of the brain circuitry involved in memory and executive function that accompanies positive motivation and engagement. (Willis, 2016)

It is not imperative that an organization pay attention to its people. Many companies aver that "our people are their greatest asset" and yet their organizational practices belie the principle. When organizations do value its people in deed as well as in word, so much more is possible; a growth mindset can flourish in place of a fixed mindset. Compliance can be supplanted by courage and innovation; resistance can be replaced by renewal. Studies are consistently showing us that employee engagement pays off in multiple ways, including bottom line results, whereas disengaged employees add to corporate overhead, negatively impact bottom lines, and reduce customer satisfaction.

So - what if we could change? What if we could leverage the natural wiring of the brain and body to create the perfect conditions for triggering the open mind and conditions necessary for learning and for generating insight and greater self-awareness? What if we could back away from the polarized confrontational mindset that threatens sensible discourse in our political and religious arenas? What if we could short-circuit the natural threat response of our brains and remake them to become collaborators and solutions-finders instead of problem-seekers and alienators? What then? How might individuals, corporations, families, societies, and nations change if we were able to create a condition of mind whereby we are open to seeing things in new ways, from the perspective of other people, and play more with ambiguity, creating solutions from a place of empathetic whole brain, whole body awareness?

What you will gain from reading this book

Whether you believe we are living in the post-modern era, or the Anthropocene Epoch, when human activities started to have a significant global impact on Earth's geology and ecosystems, humans occupying this tiny planet are living through a previously unseen, upward surge in change and complexity. It would be easy to see the 21st century as a bleak and doomed end to our evolution. Some are relying on technology to create solutions to the growing problems of over-population, climate change, energy crises, and the problem of feeding more than 7 billion people. Some are relying on the intervention of an unseen higher power. Whatever our beliefs we individuals are contributing to the outcome of this next evolutionary step without any control over the results. How can we reconcile the social and economic disparities between cultures that are still evolving out of the era of ancient history with western societies who live with unimaginably complex technologies?

Einstein said it best: "We cannot solve our problems with the same thinking we used when we created them." With the exponential growth of complexity we need exponential growth in learning, something that might be possible with the application of methods that induce us to question our assumptions, beliefs, and mental models and engage in a process of discovery of what could be from an ideal perspective – not just a better version of what is. We must venture into the land of the 'Aha' experience where invention and creativity are most at home.

The human mind is a powerful, ingenious thing. It is also dangerous when reasoning and logic are over-valued and when one lives in the so-called rational mind without the heart, stomach, and the rest of the body engaged. Brain research is showing us that the organism called human being is not made up of disparate parts; the brain sends and receives information to all parts of our bodies but is not really the director in matters associated with evaluating data and decision making. Intelligence lives in all parts of us and we ignore significant sources of internal intelligence at our peril.

We are living in times where the mind - and the 21st

century experience of living primarily in the mind - is over-valued at the expense of the rest of our being. It is as though the millions of years of evolution that created the reptilian and mammalian brain are being ignored in favour of the most recent evolutionary phase, the human brain known as the neocortex.

When we venture out into the world of work as (supposedly) rational thinking beings, it is as though we leave most of ourselves behind. We are unaware of and uneducated about how our five – yes count them five! – brains work. (Science counts as brains the processors in our hearts and stomachs in addition to the reptilian, mammalian, and neocortex brains in our heads.) (Sonnenberg & Sonnenburg, 2015)

We operate as though rationality is paramount and we tend to leave our hearts, guts, and bodies behind. Typically the results we get from this disengagement are stress, dissatisfaction in our careers, and messy relationships. We find ourselves doing things that we don't really want to be doing and that don't enrich our lives. This over-valuing of the so-called rational human underlies human conflicts on all scales, from interpersonal to global.

People are searching for solutions, for ways to reconnect with something deeply authentic. They are searching by way of spiritual paths, meditation and mindfulness, and they are searching beyond the indulgence in material satisfaction, addictions, and the pursuit of money, celebrity, and status. There are many ways to re-engage with all of our senses and become enlivened by the richness of experiencing that comes to us through our other senses. Much has been written about the integration of mind and body, about mindfulness, intuition, spiritual seeking and spiritual finding. In the workplace these topics are not usually spoken of. This book is in part designed to encourage you to find ways to speak about these things in all areas of your life, and to find ways to incorporate full physical, emotional, and psychical experiences in your daily life that will anchor you back in your body, where you belong.

Explaining the Work

Over the years that I have been doing this work I have rarely, if ever, seen someone nod their head knowingly when I tell them what I do. Instead I get blank stares or quizzical looks. It is just too far out of the normal realm for people to have encountered or be able to readily picture equine facilitated coaching in their mind's eye. Horse people don't usually understand what an executive coach does. If you are not riding a horse, then what could you possibly be doing? Business people also don't have a clue how a horse might fit into the field of executive coaching and organizational change. Most people who have heard of coaching with horses assume it is some kind of therapy. While the work is highly therapeutic, I am not a therapist and don't do therapy. So I finally decided I had to write a book that would offer enough examples and to explain to people how this works. I hope to encourage and support the movement toward valuing the contribution of the low-tech, the ancient, the slow, the complex, and the analog. Not every problem can be fixed by technology or computer science.

Another reason the work is difficult to explain is that most of what we now know about our brains has been discovered within the last few years. We have been taught a lot of myth about our brains. Not too long ago it was a canonical truth that we were born with a fixed number of brain cells and that as those died so did our brain. We now know this to be untrue. The plastic brain rewires, grows, reforms, and reconfigures itself in a way that fosters healing and learning. It is no longer gospel to assume that smart people make rational fact-based data-driven decisions; in reality our process is hidden and biased by emotions and beliefs that are based on fallacies. Our brains and bodies are highly complex and integrated, and there is immense benefit for us and society if we understood our operating systems better.

I invite you to join me on a journey through fields of personal experience, some of the latest thinking in brain/neuro science and organizational learning, and to discover the secret world of horses. I wish to introduce you to a new model of coaching individuals and organizations. I hope by the end of the book you will have had some personal 'Ahas' and perhaps experienced an opening of the mind that increases your curiosity about the world of possibilities available to those who seek instead of know. In addition I hope you are more likely to venture out of the office and into the pastures and fields where new and different ways of seeing abide.

"A mind is like a parachute. It doesn't work if it is not open."
Frank Zappa.

Introduction

"For what the horse does under compulsion ... is done without understanding; and there is no beauty in it either, any more than if one should whip and spur a dancer."
Xenophon

- One of many quotes that could be said to apply equally to people as to horses.

Unequal Partnership

When I was growing up, the stable boy at the local barn got the girl down the lane pregnant, and my future was to be forever changed. I was in love with horses from childhood but was not allowed to pursue this passion once the real danger of being around horses became clear to my parents.

To be fair to them, there was something else that kept me from connecting to horses for most of my adult life. Violence and aggression got in the way. From the time I was a small child I was highly sensitive to the look and feel of latent or overt violence and aggression. Watching cowboy movies and seeing both good and bad guys kick their horses, yank and pull the reins to make turns, spur bucking broncos until blood was drawn, and whip reins across a horse's necks and heads turned

1

me completely off. I tried a couple of times to take riding lessons as an adult and just couldn't believe that kicking a horse to make him go forward was the kind of relationship I wanted to have with that horse. Because it seemed that there was no acceptable model for the right way to treat a horse, I couldn't engage. This changed for me later, when I began to read and hear about a non-violent way to train and ride horses. As a horse trainer I know now that I wasn't in danger of hurting those horses but I believe even in my naiveté, that I was right – it was not the kind of relationship I wanted to have. If not violent, it was rude, brutish, insensitive, and disrespectful.

Humans regard horses on a wide spectrum of perspectives: from being dumb animals that need to be beaten into submission, to being spirit beings sent to help us heal and evolve to a higher evolutionary plane. The generic definition has them as livestock, used for food and other industrial by-products. Horses are too big to cuddle on your lap or to sleep on your bed and not wild enough to be considered foreign, hence they do not qualify as pets or wildlife. Interestingly, this ambiguous boundary of the familiar and the alien is where a most powerful realm of possibility lies in communicating with horses.

We share the same social requirements as horses and yet many of our primary instincts are at odds. The same human characteristics of empathy and desire for family and friends that enable us to create families and tribes we recognize in equine herds. We desire the feeling of love and connection yet as we reach out to touch a horse's head its natural desire will be to withdraw. As much as we seek the comfort of a tent or cave or house a horse will tend to avoid enclosed spaces (unless trained to living part of the time in a stall.) Our predatory instinct for capture and control of things and animals is anathema to the horses' prey instincts to be unfettered and free. Where we wish to clutch a kitten or puppy to our breast the horse will wish for the freedom to approach and withdraw as it sees fit. In fact, the whole idea of a human getting on the back of a horse and riding it is an oddity and archetype of instincts in collision. The horse innately avoids allowing something on its back and must be carefully trained to accept a rider. The human when sitting on the back of a horse is subject to the manifest power of a beast that cannot be controlled by force or logic. In fact the horse-human relationship is a testament to the power of a mythic attraction that belies logic.

That said, my approach to coaching with horses is pragmatic while allowing for the mystical to occur. In this epoch when human awareness – our sense of our own beingness - is increasingly drawn up out of our bodies and into our heads, and as we are distracted from the here and now by electronic devices and information overload, horses offer a powerful antidote and a practical way to get back into our bodies and in touch with the vast array of intelligence that is gathered by our other seven senses. Yes, I said 'other seven senses'. Dan Siegel, a medical doctor and researcher who specializes in understanding the mind, the brain, and how we can improve our experience of life, posits that we have 8 senses: the traditional 5 bodily senses, the emotional and physical sense of our body's interior, mental activities, as well as the sense of relationship or interconnectedness.

Our Horse-Human History

We have been conscripting horses into work for us for over 5000 years, much to the detriment of the horse. They have carried us on their backs as we explored the world; they pulled our chariots, ploughs, and carriages. Horses carried warriors into battle and suffered casualties and death, in equal and greater numbers alongside the cavalry and infantry. After five thousand years of 'partnering' to help bring our civilization to where it is today, in less than one hundred years they have been toppled from their place of priority and been made almost completely redundant. They have lost that special position of chief helpmate in the creation of civilization, and been relegated to a lesser role as sports equipment and entertainment. In America, the protection of the wild and mighty mustang that symbolized the cowboy spirit conquering the West is being eroded. Horses are being hunted and driven off government lands across the western plains in Canada and the US, no longer valued even as a symbol, and certainly not accorded the dignity and significance of wildlife. The 21st century global imperative that sees us consuming resources at an unparalleled rate and the demand that we put a price on everything, puts the horse square in the critical path of 21st century progress.

Horses were at one time so embedded in our culture and civilization that our language today is still peppered with expressions that come from those thousands of years of partnering: hold your horses, on the bit, on your high horse, horse of a different colour, dark horse, don't look a gift horse in the mouth, it's a horse race, back the wrong horse, track record, change horses mid-stream, put the cart before the horse, etc. Today few people ever encounter horses in the flesh. They exist in most peoples' mindscape only as a logo on a car, a building, a billboard, as a cartoon character, or as an accessory in a high fashion magazine photo.

And yet, standing on the ground next to a horse and engaging in the simplest interaction can create 'Aha' flashes as brilliant as paparazzi light bulbs. The neuroscience of the experience all adds up when one begins to investigate the powerful nature of horse-human communication and understand how our brains work.

Today we are living lives bombarded by information, much of which is marketing and propaganda. We are constantly being fed data that is increasingly curated. News and entertainment are muddled in the media. Opinions are pre-digested and fed to us by experts and carry a particular slant or vested interest that may or may not be apparent. It is becoming more and more difficult for us to separate the medium from the message, and to understand whose agenda is being promoted. We are slowly being dumbed down and increasingly distracted by data and devices.

Conversely, I hear from people every single time I get them together with a horse, that they feel better, they go deeper into themselves, they feel grounded, they connect with their own internal life like they haven't done for a very long time, they lose their fear of the power of such a large unknown animal, and they feel more alive and stimulated, sometimes for the first time in their lives.

Horses don't have an agenda other than their straight-forward need for safety, social companionship, and nourishment. Developmentally they are similar to adolescents. They require social structure. They form strong emotional bonds with other horses, humans, and other animals. They compete for affection attention, and resources. Like crows, they have long memories for individuals and distinguish between those who are friendly and those who are not.

While writing this book I met a film maker and her cameraman who needed some footage of a horse eating out of a hand. Neither of them knew much of anything about horses and had little or no prior experience. Within 5 minutes the cameraman blurted out "Wow, being around horses is so relaxing!"

At a time when we need more than ever to be present in our bodies, mindful of who we are, and how we impact other people and the environment in which we live, we are being seduced to live solely in our minds, disconnected from our feelings, physical sensations, emotional reactions, and our intuition.

Because we live in a time of an unprecedented rate of change, socially, technologically, legally, and globally, we are increasingly expected to manage our feelings, and be able to resource ourselves in order to manage our reactions to the ever constant changes around us.

Projection Screens?

Horses are sentient beings that have the power to communicate with us. With their huge wordless presence they enable us to learn a great deal about our own true natures, and help us to become present to reality in ways that are becoming increasingly rare and difficult to achieve. In order for real communication to happen however we must be prepared to see the world from their perspective and understand the way they speak to each other and to us. This is a rare occurrence but is where real richness lies.

I work with horses in a different way than others do. It is popular in the field of learning or healing with horses to posit that the horse is a screen or a mirror for our projection. I say that this is no more true than that we are screens and mirrors for each other. If we treated our friends and relations as targets for projection, we do a terrible disservice to ourselves and them. I believe it is our responsibility to understand and empathize with those with whom we interact, be they family, friends, employees, neighbours, or strangers. We need to see the differences between us and them. We must know when we are projecting our own experiences, emotions, and beliefs upon others. It is strangely myopic, narcissistic and very limiting to frame relationships as mere reflections of who we are.

For me, this difference is critical to the ethics, power, and authenticity of the work with horses. I am uncomfortable when I see people projecting their thoughts and feelings onto these silent stately beasts, who cannot refute or confirm what people claim on their behalf. Horses are and have always been highly symbolic animals. Their size and physical power alone give them a gravitas that one doesn't often encounter. When it comes to horses, size matters. They represent a near perfect screen, a tabula rasa, upon which we can impose our assumptions, beliefs, and unconscious feelings. They are unable to contradict us or 'set the record straight'.

When I started down this path I asked questions of almost everyone I met who seemed to know more than me about horses and what made them tick. Some answers I got made sense; others didn't. Sometimes I held onto information, withholding judgment until I could prove or disprove it for myself. Many horse people didn't seem to be interested in the "why" of horse behaviour. They were only interested in how to control the horse for their own ends.

There is an expression: there are some things you just can't 'unsee'. For me one of those things happened many years ago when, for the first time, I watched Canadian horse trainer and clinician Chris Irwin speak "Horse" to a horse. I have watched many clinicians and horse trainers work with horses. I sought them out because I wanted to know everything there is to know. I usually left having learned something but unimpressed with an underlying attitude of dominance mixed with a notion of the horse as utilitarian object that doesn't sit right with me.

When I first saw Chris work with a horse, I was dumbfounded. I could barely understand most of what he was explaining to us and doing with the horse, but I could see the results. He was in fact speaking to the horse in the horse's own language in direct response to what the horse was saying to him, without ever laying a hand or a whip on the horse.

In that demonstration, Chris was reading every twitch of an ear, every swish of the tail, every foot step, every turn and circle, and understood exactly what it meant to the horse and more importantly, what it said about the horse's character, and what she was telling Chris. All of this interaction was carried out on the ground without ropes, without force, and without fear from either party. (Fear is something that is demonstrated by a horse in the set of the tail and the look of the eyes.) This was not the simple round pen experience seen on TV where someone throws a rope in the direction of a horse for 15 minutes then stops and turns around and stands waiting for the horse to approach. That kind of interaction with a horse is more like a demonstration of Stockholm syndrome than true equine communication.

How do I know this? Chris was demonstrating, through awareness and clear communication, the cause and effect, the if-then of equine body language. Through a 'conversation' initiated by the horse, Chris' responses were precisely choreographed to convey to the horse "I am someone to be reckoned with, nothing to be afraid of". She tested his awareness and fitness to be in her herd until, after 20 to 25 minutes, she decided he passed her tests. Once satisfied she turned towards Chris and waited for further instructions. When asked to walk alongside him she did so, staying strictly at his shoulder, head level or low, licking her lips and chewing to signify comfort and relaxation.

I have studied with Chris for many years, and have seen many horses respond to him and his fluent way of speaking their language. It is beautiful to watch. It calls into question the validity of other horse training methods that seem designed to satisfy the requirements of humans more than the horse. The depth of understanding, the clarity and authenticity when working with horses, is essential to my values. It is simply wrong to ignore the basics of true equine communication, once you have become aware of, and understand that there is a better way.

Many organizations and individuals are finding ways to foster social conscience and responsiveness while finding ways to reduce conflict and aggression and to build bridges that span cross-cultural divides. It is my experience that the paradigm-busting effects of working with horses in this unique way helps people awaken to new perspectives, new ways of experiencing themselves and others, new ways of conceiving of interacting and of opening our minds. The neurological recipe for having "Aha" experiences is embedded in this work with horses and offers, like a prescription, a formula for creating positive, lasting change.

Part I
Equine Facilitated Executive Coaching
A Model for Individual and
Organizational Development

Chapter One - A Road Less Travelled

"The way forward is found on a path through the wilderness of the head and heart—reason and emotion. Thinking, knowing, understanding."

Laurence Gonzales, Everyday Survival: Why Smart People Do Stupid Things

Slouching Towards Markham

I drove alone across the Port Mann Bridge, leaving Vancouver British Columbia in the early morning of February 15th 1998, heading upwards towards the Rocky Mountains in the dead of winter. I had no idea what lay ahead except that I was driving 4382 kilometers east through a Canadian winter, headed for Markham, Ontario. January 1998 was the year of the ice storm of the century; I was uneasy about what kind of weather lay in front of me. The lower mainland of B.C. is the only place in Canada that isn't bone chillingly cold from November to March in any given year. Within 90 minutes of the bridge, the elevation gain on the Coquihalla Highway and the weather and road conditions were making the drive increasingly risky. I felt like an exile on the way to Siberia.

What I knew was that everything in my past to that point

had been taken away. Four years previously I had been the victim of a reorganization – and I mean victim. Despite great performance reviews and the respect of my staff and peers, I was being replaced by my new director's hand-picked wing man. It was my first exposure to the brutal vagaries of the workplace and it was a tough lesson. After losing what had been my best-ever job, I had been finding it difficult to land the next right opportunity when I was offered a great chance to go and work in the heart of Canada's IT sector in Ontario. Good opportunities on the west coast were few in those years. Although I knew it was the right thing for me, I was not exactly running with open arms and heart into a new and exciting future. I did not want to leave the beautiful west-coast ocean and mountains. I was acutely aware that my life would be irrevocably changed with this move. I knew I had a chance to create a completely new future for myself but as yet I had no idea what that would look like. The contract turned out to have many unanticipated challenges and a learning curve like the trail up to Macchu Picchu – steep, winding, sometimes heart stopping, and with poor visibility. But more on that later.

Finding myself in a new city where I knew only two people, I needed to find something special to occupy my off-work hours. I hate going to the gym and am not much of a sports fan. I wanted to do something outdoorsy and I remembered that I had always wanted to take the fabled horseback vacation in the Rockies. I decided it was time to learn how to ride a horse so that, when the time came, I wouldn't spend the whole trip panicked and fearful. This was only three years after Christopher Reeve's widely publicized fluke riding accident that left him a quadriplegic and I was past the age of feeling immortal.

I located a barn that was relatively close to where I was

living and signed up for a lesson. Part of the first lesson was learning how to tack up the horse. I was standing to the left of my instructor, closest to the horse's head. As she was explaining the girth fitting to me and tightening it, the horse reached around and bit my arm. I mistakenly took this as a bad omen. The lesson turned out to be both terrifying and exhilarating. The instructor barked out commands and exhortations that reminded me of a blending of ballet and sailing lessons. My body was being asked to assume completely unnatural positions that worked against all my natural instincts while the equipment, upon which my life depended, had foreign obscure names that were meaningless to me. I didn't know how to operate it and I was afraid I was going to die if I didn't use the 'whatsit' the right way.

When I dismounted at the end of that first lesson and my foot touched the ground, I was overwhelmed by the sensations of having activated parts of my being that felt like they hadn't been lit up for years. It was like having a deep tissue massage of my psyche, my spirit, my intuition, and my whole physiology. I was aware that, although I could not yet put into words what had happened to me, this was a powerful internal experience and I wanted to do it again, be able to share it, and to be able to create it for others. In that moment, my next career goal was set: to foster personal and professional development and self-awareness through being fully present with horses.

It took many years for me to be able to articulate that experience. In 1998 equine-assisted coaching or learning was a little-known field with few practitioners and there were no guideposts to help me find a way forward. I was drawn by an innate understanding that the horses were helping reconnect me to my intuition and that, by following this inner magnetic north, I would find my teachers and my way. Over the course of the following years I learned as much as I could from everyone I encountered who claimed to have expertise with horses. As I paid close attention to my own inner voice and developed my skill as a rider and horsewoman, I learned to trust my intuition again.

At the same time I was measuring what I was learning with the horses against the daily experiences in my new workplace. The partners were looking to me to drive the implementation and acceptance of a new system for which there was a lot of resistance. The company was a business partner of IBM. The changes that the partners were trying to implement were creating upheaval in the ranks. There was a perception of a leadership void that was stirring up competitive energy resulting in occasional outbursts of ego-driven unproductive behaviour which added to the stress and anxiety about the, as yet, unknown future. I have always believed that "all behaviour makes sense" and that oftentimes we just needed to put more effort into uncovering the motivation of people when their actions seemed mysterious or unaccountable. The behaviours at work started to make more sense to me when I compared them to the behaviour of horses.

Social Animals, Social Brains

Being part of a herd demands certain skills and abilities in order to succeed. Science is investigating what is called the social brain of the human as well as other animals. (Goleman, 2007) The social brain is the part of the brain that is aware of its environment and how to interact with it, the awareness of other beings and how to relate to them, as well as the awareness of self. Horses appear not to be in the category of animals that have self-awareness the way dolphins and many primates do (recognizing themselves in a mirror). However their social brains have evolved to understand their environments and the minds or feelings of other beings. This accounts for their ability to interpret the intentions of humans and other creatures and likely accounts for their odd propensity to form bonds with humans and allow us to join their herds.

Most horse owners will attest to the fact that horses anticipate and intuit the intentions of people. Clever Hans is a legendary horse that lived at the end of the 19th and early 20th century. He appeared to respond to spoken and written requests from his owner providing answers to mathematical questions, questions about dates, how to read and spell, and to identify people by matching pictures to their printed names. An investigation later determined that Clever Hans was responding to micro-movements made by his owner that were below the level of consciousness of the owner himself as well as audiences. In other words the horse could see and interpret the tiniest of indicators from his owner of what or when the correct response was reached. The discerning senses of the horse could read his human more intensively than another human. (This topic of micro expressions and how to read them is a new area of research being pursued by Paul Ekman and others. The output of this kind of research is aimed at understanding the science of emotions, how to read and manage emotions, and how to know when people are being emotionally congruent – or not.)

As I learned about the primal needs of the horses - for social position and security, for predictability in leadership and assertiveness over territorial disputes – I could see more clearly what was going on between people in the workplace. I saw and began to understand that, with people, words and actions could be diametrically opposed and the sometimes uncomfortable-feeling-in-the-pit-of-my-stomach was actually intelligence to which I ought to pay closer attention. Gradually I began to make more of the sense that people were making even when their words and behaviour were at odds.

The Great Delusion - the Rational Mind

I was seeing in myself and the people around me the active delusion that we, of the dorsolateral prefrontal cortex (go on, google it), are rational creatures making decisions based solely on data and facts. In reality our decision making capabilities are influenced by our emotions much more than we realize. We live in our minds, often in what is called the default mode network (Buckner, 2008), in the past and the future, parsimoniously permitting selective awareness of minimal sensory input, looking for patterns and categories, matching memories to current conditions, predicting outcomes instead of actually living them, largely unaware of most of the input being processed by our systems in the moment. We spend much of our time in an unreal abstract world.

> "Human beings spend nearly all of their time in some kind of mental activity, and much of the time their activity consists not of ordered thought but of bits and snatches of inner experience: daydreams, reveries, wandering interior monologues, vivid imagery, and dreams. These desultory concoctions, sometimes unobtrusive but often moving, contribute a great deal to the style and flavor of being human." (Klinger, 1971)

It is no wonder that we increasingly thirst for relief from this internal abstraction and seek answers in yoga, meditation, spiritual and religious pursuits. What I was learning from the horses was a kind of sanity and sense of being at home within myself that had been eluding me. I did not yet know much about brains, the physiology of intuition, electro-magnetic fields or affect contagion. However I was unconsciously connecting to horses and people not just as a human but as a mammal. Working for a company in the field of information technology, a totally abstract and disconnected-from-real-life field of endeavor, I was experiencing the differences between the way we humans interact and the way equines interact with each other and with people. The similarities were surprising. The differences were highly instructive. Watching the horses compete for status and resources was simulated every day in the office. As I became more curious and observant about the horses, I developed a new ability to observe non-verbal behaviours with people while paying attention to their words. I found the humans very much more complex than the horses, which led me to be more curious about motivations.

The company was going through a high degree of change, repositioning itself in a more competitive market, and overhauling its business model. The organizational culture was at a low level of maturity and in order to succeed and meet its growth goals, the company had to make some substantial and painful decisions. As the pressure increased, behaviour deteriorated at all levels of the company. It was the first time I witnessed such stark differences in the value and impact of hard and soft skills. In an industry where technical and engineering skills were considered essential, hard skills, devoid of accompanying 'soft' skills, were almost useless.

It was part of my job to engage the partners in strategic planning regarding organizational culture as well as other structural changes. I watched some personnel fail at understanding the compelling need to adapt and change. As a consultant it was much easier for me to stand apart and support the change process but it was on occasion, like watching a train wreck. As someone who has always sought to assist people to find their niche, I reveled in the successes of those who could align themselves to the new reality, and I felt very badly for those who could not.

Having been through such a similar painful reorganizational change myself, I related to the way our minds and emotions can sabotage us. I was experiencing changes within myself that I would have not thought possible previously and part of what seemed to be accelerating the change was the time I was spending with the horses. With the horses I was experiencing a different mindset than I had previously been exposed to. It wasn't just the intensity of the focus – I was used to that from many other passions I had enjoyed in life such as music, art, and in some of my previous jobs. I was experiencing an intense kind of self-reflection and evaluation that was less judgmental and more instructive.

It was in these days that I learned how important relationships are to horses. I got to observe the intense friendships and rivalries that horses have that were replicated every day by people at work. I observed how these relationships can be formed and how they can be broken. In the office, the organizational changes were fracturing some long-standing friendships. Some were forever altered. Trust was lost and in some cases would never be regained.

As new people were hired who were more aligned with the company's new direction the social fabric of the organization had to be rewoven. Alliances shifted and power was reallocated. The behaviours were not at all unlike what I observed as the horses at the stable were changed. New horses had to find their place in the social structure and hierarchy. A horse who once was always first at the water trough was no longer first. Observing the invisible mantle of power and influence at work in the equine herd was almost indistinguishable from the human herd at work. The similarities between us two-legged mammals and the four legged ones were highly instructive and served to help me disengage from the drama while staying curious and engaged with the reality of what was happening in the office.

Chapter Two - Organizational Culture and How We Shape it.

"Culture eats strategy for breakfast."
Peter Drucker

"I came to see, in my time at IBM, that culture isn't just one aspect of the game, it is the game. In the end, an organization is nothing more than the collective capacity of its people to create value."
Louis Gerstner, IBM

Organizational Culture: What Is It and Why Does It Matter

Over the years I have been a member of many barn communities, each with its own unique written and unwritten rules or codes of behaviour and sense of place. What I have seen in these barns is that, humans or horses, we mammals all have input. Like a yawn, emotions are contagious and their progression through a group, be it herd or office, is viral, predictable, and yet often ineffable. We horses and humans are social animals and as we create a herd, a family, a tribe or community, temporarily or for long periods of time, we each contribute to the ambient mood or character of the whole through the energy, beliefs, behaviour, and emotional responses we have to everyday occurrences.

As we humans observe the orchestrated movement of a flock of songbirds on the wing or a school of fish dodging a predator, we marvel at the invisible communication that enables the whole to move as one entity without a single collision. Put us in a cubicle farm or an office and we soon forget that the same invisible orchestration is occurring to us and is generated by us. We create our environment every moment; the creation of a great organizational culture will be entirely dependent on our ability to own our contributions.

Organizational culture is typically described as a system of shared assumptions, values, and beliefs, which govern how people behave in organizations. These shared values and beliefs have a strong influence on the people in the organization and dictate how they dress, act, and perform their jobs. Affect contagion, the emotional input to the group, is generally not acknowledged in discussions of organizational culture but is significant to the felt sense of any culture.

There is an insightful article in the Harvard Business Review about the science of building great organizational culture through building great teams. (Pentland, 2012) The research findings of a group from MIT's Human Dynamics Laboratory show how wireless sensory devices worn by teams of people were able to capture more than 100 data points per minute about the complex communication cues that pass among people that work together. By documenting tone of voice, physical positioning with each other, how much each person talked, listened, gestured, or interrupted, and by comparing the results to objective performance measures such as financial results or customer service metrics, the authors were able to define factors of interaction that produce high-performing teams and in addition, were able to predict success based on these factors. Although the author doesn't explicitly say so, I believe the data points did not include communication content – only the non-language points of communication.

The researchers boiled the results down to three factors that are fundamental to success in teams: energy (the number and nature of exchanges among teams), engagement (the distribution of energy among teams), and exploration (communication that team members have with others outside of the team). One of the interesting findings was that in-person communication was found to be the most valuable form of communication, with phone and video-conference taking second and third place. Email and texting were found to be the least valuable form of communication. Dare we deduce that the physicality of a person's presence, even if by voice over the phone, is the key differentiator for effective communication?

A big part of the territory we explore in equine facilitated executive coaching is the realm of the non-verbal. Working without spoken language during exchanges with horses enables us to really experience and focus on the non-verbal ways we communicate. The energy we bring to an interaction, the raising of eyebrows, the hint of a smile or a frown, the slight thrust of a shoulder: these are all signals that speak volumes to horses, but usually slip past our conscious awareness. The 100 plus data points captured in the MIT study mentioned above are too complex for our linguistically-oriented brains to keep track of, but these cues will not slip past the notice of your average horse. Their very survival depends upon their ability to see in minute detail what information - non-verbal signals - from others can tell them.

In fact, just like in the workplace, when our leaders communicate with mixed messages, behave in rude or insensitive ways, we humans exhibit the same kind of compensating behaviours that horses do. We either shut down, become passive, passive–aggressive, or we act out and challenge authority. We as leaders cannot communicate effectively to all the people all of time, but we can all certainly make strides to improve our emotional awareness, our non-verbal behaviour, improve our ability to understand when our messaging is not landing with people, and find ways to reach others with clear, effective, heart-felt communication.

Monkey See, Monkey Do

"This process in which a person or a group influences the emotions and affective behavior of another person or group through the conscious or unconscious induction of emotions is referred to as emotional contagion (EC)" (Sherrie Bourg Carter, 2012)

That emotion is contagious is a physiological fact. We now know more of the underlying mechanisms that generate the transmission of states of being such as mirror neurons, and yet the impact this invisible way of communicating has on us is rarely part of our consciousness. In fact, people not only unconsciously mimic the behaviours of others but we also feel the same feelings.

Affect contagion or emotional contagion is an essential part of human communication; it is a result of physical activation - a sympathetic proto-communication. This affect contagion forms the underlying feeling state of an organization's culture in the same way it does a herd. It is really, simply put, the chemical communication of emotions from one being to another.

I have worked in a number of large post-secondary institutions. The overall mood or affect of these places is influenced heavily by the youthful energy of the student population. One department sticks out in my mind because the organizational climate that one encountered when one walked through the office door was powerfully different, like hitting a brick wall. Every time I went into the office area I wondered what it was that generated the discomfort I felt. It was impossible to put a finger on it. The main symptoms were that people behind the counter didn't seem to have warm genuine smiles. The sound was muted; people were talking in very low voices as though we were in a funeral home. Given the role that this office played in the marketing of the university I found it strange and discordant. Eventually I asked a few colleagues what their impression was of the mood and there seemed to be agreement about a slightly uncomfortable ambience. It became apparent through subsequent reorganizations that the mood was an affect that flowed from the leader of the department. When the leader changed so did the feeling.

We talk about energy all the time but often we don't pay attention to it; the information is useful to help to leverage change in groups or organizations. Leaving emotions out of the conversation and addressing change from only an intellectual perspective limits our chances for success. When organizations are at their most healthy the affect will reveal it. The energy will be congruent with feelings of satisfaction, respect, trust, safety, and the sense of well-being that comes from people who feel valued, who feel safe, and who know their purpose. That leaders have a huge part in creating and affecting the ambient emotional mood of organizations is a phenomena that is not, in my experience, adequately recognized and accounted for in organizational change management.

In organizational change management, best practices dictate that you have a well-defined business case, a project plan, a communication plan, a governance structure, a vision for the future, top down leadership that champions and communicates consistently about the change, and a plan for keeping key stakeholders informed and engaged. It is atypical to have a component of the planning dedicated to managing resistance and recognizing the emotional reactions and stressors resulting from change initiatives. Coaching is an important adjunct tool for ensuring success in change projects because it is an obvious arena in which to explore these topics.

The conventional wisdom is that 70% of change initiatives fail. (It is difficult to demonstrate proof of these statistics especially when we don't have access to the definitions of success that are attached to the 70%.) Nevertheless, it has been my experience in managing and participating in many change initiatives that the outcomes are never quite as envisioned and are, often as not, regarded as failures by many of the people who are impacted by the change.

An article in the Huffington Post from 2013 (Dea, 2013) lists the three reasons change management fails:

- Reason Number 1: Change consultants are insufficiently equipped on a personal level.
- Reason Number 2: Most change models are incomplete.
- Reason Number 3: Capacity is widely overlooked, on all levels,

Ultimately, the reasons above boil down to insufficient attention paid to the human resources. Dea discusses the problems and struggles of people's ability to have the personal breakthroughs required to embrace and transform themselves and others as part of a change initiative. It is common for leadership to underestimate the capacity of people to accept, embrace, and continually drive change, juggling the old and the new during the life of the change. The capacity for people to resist change and be stuck in old ways of doing things can and will infect change programs at all levels of the organization.

Changing minds is hard work. I believe it is impossible to change minds without changing bodies and by that I mean dealing with the emotional content of the threats associated with change and finding novel and constructive ways to engage people in exploring that which they wish to avoid. People learn and change by finding new things themselves - in their own way and in their time. People need to discover that new thing. Being shown it and told it simply doesn't work well.

Awareness is a key skill in recognizing the signs and symptoms of change resistance. Learning and applying the lessons of neuroscience, we can tackle resistance more effectively and leverage the potential of the new being seen to be desired, or at least less threatening. Coaching with horses can circumvent the so-called rational pre-frontal cortex, whose mission is to identify threats and avoid them, even when they are not real. Working with groups or with individuals in equine facilitated sessions can move people into territory where change is not an either-or situation. Coaching with horses creates space for people to have their own creative break-throughs and find ways to integrate challenges and threats by connecting with their innermost deep personal power.

"Neuroscientists have found that only through bombarding the brain with new experiences do we force our minds to look at the world through a new lens. That means you need to get out of the office once in a while." (Carmine Gallo, 2014)

Chapter Three - Awareness and Presence; Fundamentals for Leadership

"What makes you think human beings are sentient and aware? There's no evidence for it. Human beings never think for themselves, they find it too uncomfortable. ... The characteristic human trait is not awareness but conformity, and the characteristic result is religious warfare.
Other animals fight for territory or food; but, uniquely in the animal kingdom, human beings fight for their 'beliefs.'"
Michael Crichton, The Lost World

Awareness

Some months into my development and progress as a novice rider, I had a sudden realization. I had not yet heard the expression "ride every step" but after riding several different horses and becoming slowly less incompetent, it suddenly dawned upon me that I would never get this or any horse onto the bit, going at the right gait in the right direction at the right speed, and then have him or her carry on from there so that

I could switch to autopilot and not work so hard. I realized that up until that moment I had been doing what I tended to do whenever I was in a struggle to acquire new knowledge or skills. Despite the fact that I love learning, I wanted to learn enough to become competent and knowledgeable so that I could relax and enjoy myself, and go back to into my comfort zone and effectively check out.

Suddenly I knew that this horse and I were in a real relationship - a dance in which I had to stay continuously engaged, communicating, listening, speaking, and dancing every note and every step with him. I suddenly realized that the horse was engaged and communicating with me ALL the time and that I was selling him short by giving only part of myself to this relationship. What a wake-up call. Right then I made the commitment to stay in the moment and I began to fall in love with that horse. The whole experience became a new kind of pleasure of being truly present in the moment, living in the ambiguity of not knowing and knowing all at the same time.

In that lesson I started to realize that this was the model for more mindful human interaction. The tiny movements, involuntary and voluntary, that reveal our internal states are mostly missed. As we focus inwardly on our thoughts and words, we tend to miss the input that is in front of our eyes. We relate in a state of half duplex – as they say in telecom speak - we are sending and receiving at the same time but we are not able to be conscious of both simultaneously.

It turns out we actually cannot multi-task. Our brains move from input to output, past to present to future, listening to part of what is being said and then cutting out to prepare a response, noticing and processing emotional reactions and determine what is safe to reveal in this current relationship in the current moment. We create and edit language and thoughts while remaining largely unconscious of the body and non-verbal cues that betray our internal condition. We are often interacting with ghosts; the people we think we know are represented symbolically in our minds and it is often that representation that we are speaking and engaging with, rather than the fully alive conscious and autonomous being in whose presence we stand.

This appears contrary to the way horses communicate and socialize. As prey animals they are mostly non-verbal, communicating with large and small physical gestures. Being without a complex spoken language, horses have elevated the art of communication through non-verbal means. Heightened awareness of the most minute signals of the internal states of others makes horses much more astute than us, enabling them to interact and remain in the present with full emotional awareness.

Detached and Non-Reactive Awareness

Awareness is such an inconsequential and impotent word to describe a facility as critical to our beingness as the power of awareness; we give it very little thought. What does it mean to be aware? Is it the same thing as being conscious or sentient? Is it the same as mindfulness? Is awareness really much more about conformity in behaviour as Michael Crichton suggests in the quote above?

Consciousness is generally accepted to be a synonym for awareness: to know oneself and one's surroundings, to know others, to have memory, and to be able to conceive of a future. To be sensible in the old fashioned meaning of the word would be a good equivalent to being conscious - which is to say to be rational and of sound mind.

Awareness, in the sense I am describing, is more a

heightened state of consciousness or sensibility. Awareness can be said to be greater than mindfulness or meditation because when we are aware we are capable of detecting change. The more aware we are, the more input we are able to perceive.

Tibetan Buddhist meditation master Chogyam Trungpa says: "Mindfulness is like a microscope; it is neither an offensive nor a defensive weapon in relationship to the germs we observe through it. The function of the microscope is just to present clearly what is there." (Trungpa, 2004)

To be in a state of mindfulness or meditation is to be focused on something, blocking out the surroundings. When mindful, our sensory apparatus is still detecting sound, smell, touch, and possibly taste but the conscious mind is filtering out non-essential information. Our attention is on a focal point – our breath, a candle, a sound, a physical sensation.

Awareness is in the sense I am describing is to have diffuse attention that can move in and out of focus, shifting from the internal states of our own being to the whole environment in which we exist, to the observation and evaluation of the other sentient beings in our presence. A heightened level of awareness permits the proverbial chopping of wood and carrying of water while experiencing the benefits of paying attention without attachment and reactivity. To be fully aware and yet detached and non-reactive to sensory input is be in a special state of heightened awareness. This I believe is the way horses live, for the most part. This is the way we can be and ought to be with horses; this type of awareness promotes bonding and helps to create safety for us humans while being in the presence of large flight animals with more powerful sensitivities than ours.

The wonderful side effect for people who participate in this enriched communing with horses is the mental capacity-building that occurs; we practice and build mastery in the ability to live in the present moment with enhanced levels of awareness. Neuroplasticity tells us that our brains are literally being changed by this type of focused activity.

Sleepwalking in the Information Age

Daniel Siegel and other scientists are digging deeply into the topics of mindfulness, awareness, happiness, and perception. There is a great deal of interest in these topics in corporate circles such as Google, Intel, and General Mills about how to increase productivity and employee wellness through meditative practices. I doubt that this is coincidental with the increasing levels of mindlessness and unconsciousness we experience in our distracted worlds. What we seem to be doing is paying attention to more information but ironically perceiving less. We feel as that, even as we are taking in more information, our attention span is shrinking.

The three zones of awareness, as I call them, are the internal - the self, the environmental, and the zone of the other. The awareness of self includes that knowledge of one's emotional state as it fluctuates and shifts, as well as one's physical and mental states. In order to be truly aware, we need to be able to flex our awareness muscles and stretch both out and in at the same time. Like the horse, who is maintaining vigilance of the environment and others at all times in order to enhance the chance of survival, we benefit from having a neutral centered sense of all three zones at once. We cannot truly multi-task but I have found it possible when I am with the horses, to single-task on a grander scale, maintaining an enlarged sphere of awareness and space in which my attention can float, taking in and noting the changes that go on around me, while remaining non-reactive to any one thing – unless it is presenting danger to myself or others.

What is fundamental to any state of mind or body is

what is happening with our energetic selves. Whether we are conscious of it or not, our bodies are made up of energy that

The Sphere of Awareness

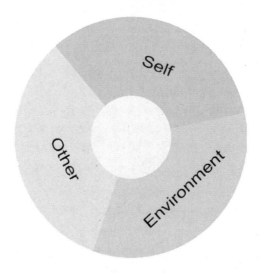

is synchronous with our emotional state and is perceptible to others. The energetic body is an emerging area of scientific research, some of it made possible by new and powerful imaging tools and techniques such as fMRI (functional magnetic resonance imaging) and EMF (electro-magnetic field) detectors.

What in the sixties was referred to as one's "aura" or "vibe" turns out to be based in scientific fact. We are all energetic beings that emit information invisibly to each other - invisibly but not unnoticed. That unspoken and hard-to-describe "vibe" is a function of energy being transmitted and received by parts of our bodies that don't process language and thus make it difficult for us to articulate and comprehend. When we are living an experience dominated by the left hemisphere we are less capable of being aware of energy and the communication of information via the energetic field.

Research by scientists sponsored by the Heart Math Institute is producing some interesting results in terms of being able to measure the existence of, and the means of influencing, the human body's electro-magnetic field. (Mccraty) This is an area where the language of equines excels. Over millions of years of evolution, the horses' survival has depended, not on verbal language or audible communication - for they are a relatively silent species, but on being able to see and read energy and intention and on being able to communicate with each other instantaneously by way of energy and body language. The work that we do as equine facilitated coaches, in part, is to assist in fostering self-awareness and learning from the feedback available to us in the communication with horses. To be working with horses is almost like working with EMF detectors. We get instantaneous feedback about our energetic selves as well as our non-verbal physical signals.

Phantom – Awareness in Action

Early morning mist was lifting gently off the pasture. It was Saturday and I was mucking out Phantom's paddock and stall as usual. He had been a little jumpy since I arrived. There was a light breeze and I knew enough to recognize that with the limitations of my homo sapien's sensory apparatus, there was likely a lot more going on in Phantom's universe than I would ever know. The same light breeze that felt refreshing to me could be carrying sounds and smells to his more sensitive ears and nose that might be more threatening than pleasant. The meaning he was making of sensory input would be specific to his equine physiology, his evolutionary history, his own personal past, and his current world view.

He was a relative newcomer to this herd and, as with most

captive horses, was living in a space surrounded by fence rails that restricted his critical flight distance. He wasn't able to truly test his herd mates to see who was who in the hierarchy. If predators appeared his best mode of defense, running away, would be unavailable to him. Unless he could jump the fence and make a run for it, he would be forced to stand and fight, something that horses are not generally inclined to want to do. His paddock was reasonably large by local standards but paddocks are more prison than home to horses. Phantom was a horse that pretended to be a leader. He was a dominant type, always testing and pushing the boundaries, giving the impression that he was in charge.

Suddenly a horse in the next field bolted. Phantom instantly reacted and charged from his paddock into his stall, turned and charged out again. His eyes were wide and staring, his nostrils were flaring, and he was snorting for good measure. Without thinking I sauntered over to the fence between Phantom and the other horse. I leaned against the fence and assumed a stance of total relaxation and calm. I blew air out of my mouth letting my lips flap, mimicking the sound horses make when they blow off stress. Phantom stopped running in an out of his stall, looked over visibly curious, and almost instantly started to relax. His eyes softened, his nostrils shrank back to their normal size. He blew a few more times and then slowly he walked over to me and stood close to the fence, letting his head drop, a sure sign of the onset of relaxation. We silently shared territory, together as allies.

What happened in that moment with Phantom was something I learned from being with the horses over many years. I had almost without knowing it been building up my awareness muscles. Like a horse, I was becoming used to paying attention to my inner state, my environment, as well as the emotional state of those in my presence – both horse and human. I had been developing the hyper-awareness of the prey animal and it was becoming an habitual part of my experience with them.

Not only was I paying more constant attention, I was living so much more in the moment that I had become much less reactive such that when Phantom bolted I processed the information available to me; I made a split-second decision that previously I likely would have been unable to make in a timely manner for Phantom's benefit. I would probably have startled at Phantom's obvious fear and my internal alarms would have escalated, my reaction exciting Phantom even more, his escalation getting me more fearful and stressed – the true full-on amygdala response and affect contagion. The phenomena of affect contagion would have had us both stressed for no apparent reason. Instead, in that moment I recognized Phantom's need for leadership, for someone to let him know that he wasn't alone, and that I could be relied upon to know what he needed and provide safety for him. His reaction, coming closer with a low head and blowing off his stress, demonstrated he was having his needs met.

Practicing awareness is one of the essential steps to developing a consciousness that is more evolved than the self-interested consciousness that our older brains condemn us to. We may not escape our reptilian brains but we need not be condemned to live at the end of the amygdala's leash. Through the application of focus and attention and exposure to the states of heightened awareness we can develop the habit of non-reactivity and emotional stability that fosters creativity, harmony, and greater effectiveness in groups and teams.

Presence

"The most precious gift we can offer others is our presence."
Thich Nhat Hanh

Working with Matt

I was working with two clients who were wanting to practice their equine body language. We were going to work with a horse named Matt in a round pen. I knew the horse quite well. He was a well-adjusted reliable guy, and although there was nothing complicated about his personality, there was something complicated about his breed. He was a Tennessee Walker, a gaited horse whose movement was difficult for many people to ride. Matt was also highly sensitive to the physical stress that a rider might feel while struggling to find a way to sit his peculiar way of going. Matt's response to the stress was simple – he eliminated it by dumping his rider. It wasn't long before Matt had a reputation and, like many horses who are a challenge to people, he was at risk of becoming an agricultural by-product. Matt was lucky because he met a woman who knew how to understand his special needs and with time and attention, and because she knew how to speak his language, he ended up in the right job with the right person. Being a calm and respectful horse he was well-suited to working on the ground in the kind of work I do.

Both clients were going to have some one-on-one time in the round pen with Matt. The first client went in and, using some basic body language and energetic self-control was able to have Matt stand as she approached him, was able to send him on, leading from behind, using just her energy and body language, and finally, was able to have him walk with her shoulder to shoulder around the round pen for a few circuits. Matt spoke to her with his ears, his licking and chewing lips, his low head and his calm slightly lifted tail, letting her know that he was enjoying her presence. She was elated when she was done.

The second client went in and slowly walked towards his shoulder. Matt froze. He didn't stand there waiting for her to join him – he froze. He was on alert, ears swiveled towards her as she walked towards him. His eyes widened and had a look of stress as his tail clamped slightly. The client arrived at Matt's shoulder and stood there for a few minutes. Then she started to ask him to walk forward with her. Matt would not move. His behaviour was completely unlike the way he had interacted with client number one. I asked the client what was going on for her. She indicated that nothing was going on, everything was fine. I was at a distance so that I could not tell how her breathing was or see the micro-expressions in her face. She seemed to be 'fine' and yet she could not get Matt to walk with her. She continued to ask. Suddenly he leapt forward and walked purposefully around in front of her. As they drew nearer to where I was standing I asked again what was going on for the client. She confessed that the knots in her stomach had softened and now she was feeling less afraid. I coached her to breathe and relax as much as possible and eventually Matt was able to slow down and be with her as they walked around the pen.

Horses are so adept at feeling what is going on for others. They never fail to show us what their experience of us is. Despite the fact that I couldn't see the fear and stress in the client's body, Matt could feel it at a distance and was unable to relax and be with the client until she could acknowledge her feelings and begin to let them go.

"You don't get a second chance to make a first impression," says James Uleman, PhD, a psychology professor at New York University and researcher on impression management. "In spite of the congeniality of many professional gatherings, judgments are being made and impressions formed all the time." First impressions are an example of our presence at a particular moment in time. Substantial research has affirmed the importance of first impressions while exploring a variety of factors that contribute to their formation. For example, a 2009 study in Personality and Social Psychology Bulletin found that factors ranging from clothing style to posture play a role in how impressions are formed. (Rowh, 2012)

Presence is not quite the same thing as impression. Presence is not about the clothes you wear or your handshake. It is much more about your emotional affect, your energy level, your non-verbal communication and your mental state. Presence is mutable. Much of our presence is unconscious and involuntary but we do have the ability to affect our presence with our mood, our body language, our mental and emotional state, and our level of energy.

I submit that the most lasting part of the impression one makes is the felt sense of who we are.

Presence is an overloaded term; it has many different meanings and connotations. It means many things – often we think of presence is terms of being somewhere – in opposition to being absent. We are each of us present somewhere in space at this very moment. At this very moment who else is present with you? What is the quality of your experience of that other person or persons who share space with you right now? Is there a quality of the space as a result of the absence of others?

Imagine someone you love. Bring that person into your mind and imagine that person being present with you right now. What happens to the quality of your experience? Now imagine someone that you really do not get along with or actually really dislike. What is the quality of your experience and how is it changed?

These abstract conceptions are representations of your felt experience, memories of the quality of your reality that are created or altered by the presence of these other people. Now, think about these other people, imagine what their experience might be if they were to do this same experiment conjuring you into their mind's eye. Their experience will be their recollection of you and your presence. Presence is a very real experience; it's not just a memory but this kind of remembering demonstrates just how powerful presence is.

A Bodyprint

We all have a presence that is a unique as our fingerprints but for the most part we're unaware of it. Others know us by our presence. Presence is what is missed by our loved one when we are absent. It is a critical factor in our lives because it is the 'who' we declare ourselves to be in the world and how we are known, more so than by our name.

How can someone use this information to their advantage? How can you moderate and change your presence to achieve your ends? As with anything, having the awareness that your presence may not be serving you at all times is the starting point. Having the awareness to notice how people react to your presence and, more importantly, being able to adjust your presence in the moment, and see and understand the results you achieve can be a powerful way to manage your presence. Developing awareness of your emotional state, your mental state, and your energetic state in the moment is a skill worth developing and is that starting point to being able to moderate your presence.

Stepping Up for Cricket

We stepped into the round pen with Cricket, a beautiful black Quarter Horse with an alpha mare presence. My client, whom I will call Sonia, was diminutive and her disposition was on the quiet side. If you walked into a room and she was there with a few other people you might not notice her right away. She tended to recede into the background. Nevertheless this woman was not without humour, intellect, and gumption. For a woman of her size she showed real grit when she entered the round pen to be with this 1100 pound creature called Cricket.

As we stood inside by the gate talking about her goal for the sessions, Cricket impatiently walked off to the left. She went up against the wall of the round pen fencing and walked purposefully, following the fencing around the circle. Inevitably she came around to where we were standing. I watched her approach and made sure my client was aware of her as well. I had worked with this horse many times and had never seen her behave this way before.

Cricket walked up to my client and stopped almost nose to nose with Sonia. Sonia shrank back with her hands up against her chest and look of great surprise on her face. After a few seconds Cricket moved off and took another clockwise walk around the round pen. I asked Sonia, how she felt about this and checked in with her to make sure she felt safe, and that she knew I would intervene if necessary. Sonia, although a little shaken, was prepared to stand her ground. Cricket came around again and the two repeated their actions, Cricket stopping just short of Sonia's nose and Sonia shrinking back and holding her hands up to her chest again in a 'Stop' pose.

Again, Cricket waited not a full moment before she headed off again. Clearly she had something on her mind that had to do specifically with Sonia. After the first confrontation, I asked my client if this was in any way similar to her relationships and she concurred that indeed it was. She often felt disrespected, unacknowledged, and sometimes intimidated. As Cricket was coming around for the third time I asked my client what she could do to change that behaviour and have Cricket respect her. Sonia prepared herself and put up a block by extending her hands out with straight arms. In that movement she changed her energy to make herself seem bigger and feel more powerful. Cricket stopped about three feet from Sonia and then walked off. Thus ended the lesson.

There are many horse people who think that horses read our energy. Just like the hippie's idea of 'vibes' and auras, horses appear to be able to detect, by feel or by sight or a combination, whatever energetic information we emit. Whatever it is that horses are sensing from us and other beings, it has been key to their survival as a species. When we can understand their responses to us we can get valuable honest feedback, the like of which is not possible to get from other people.

Awareness and presence are fundamental to the qualities of good leadership. Some leaders are born with these qualities and others must develop them. They are not acquired in a classroom, online, or with the mind alone. They can be learned from experiential activities and can be developed by being in relationship with trusted colleagues, friends, mentors, advisors, and, dare I say, horses. Being open to good quality feedback that comes from trusted sources is invaluable.

Chapter Four - What Have Horses Got to Do With It?

Giving Harold the Finger

During the first few years of my pursuit of knowledge about horses and after working with coaches, trainers, and clinicians, I had gotten over the idea that horses were dumb beasts. The notion that horses did not have feelings and existed to serve us for transportation, war, agriculture or sport didn't wash in the 21st century. I was coming to see that horses understood us better than we understood them, that they had language, and that they likely assumed we knew what we were saying to them with our bodies when in fact we were, for the most part, completely oblivious.

I had accepted that pulling horses along at the end of a halter of bridle would be considered rude to a horse and I had learned how to move a horse without pulling. The rest was still vague theory when one day I was in Harold's stall getting him cleaned and tacked up for a ride. The stall was the usual size – about 130 square feet. I stood at the door and without thinking turned around and bent over to retrieve something from his grooming kit. At the bottom of the bend I suddenly heard a loud crash coming from behind me. I quickly stood up straight and whirled around to see Harold backed up against the wall with a look of fright on his face. The whites of enlarged eyes were visible and the wrinkles around them were pronounced. He had backed right into the wall which accounted for the crash. Suddenly I became aware that I had just effectively given him the finger if not outright threatened him by showing him my backside. Horses turn their back ends to other horses to warn them that a kick is coming and to get them to back off. Harold of course had nowhere to go so my action was not just sudden and uncalled for but uncaring in that he was boxed in and literally up against the wall. I had just been, in horse terms, extremely thoughtless and rude.

In coaching it is often said that we meet the client where they are. There doesn't appear to be a set of hard and fast rules or fixed parameters on how to 'meet clients' where they are. What that looks like will vary from client to client and coach to coach and be entirely dependent upon personality and life circumstances. In essence a coach attempts to understand her client's values, beliefs, and interests and does not require a client to meet some arbitrary qualifications in order to be coached. It is fundamental to coaching that we regard clients as whole, complete, and not in need of fixing. Incorporating a client's learning style, world view, and mental models is important for a coaching engagement to succeed. Once a suitability for a coaching relationship has been determined, a coaching contract can be agreed. I apply these same principles not just to the people I coach but also to the horses I work with.

What does it mean to meet horses where they are? Having studied horses for the requisite 10,000 hours I have come to understand some things about them that have informed my approach to them and how I coach with them. Not everyone shares the same beliefs about horses, religion, or politics so I expect some may, and likely will, disagree with some of my ideas.

It is important for equine facilitated executive coaching that the horses who coach with me are suited to the work. Not all are. I interview them before accepting them as co-coaches. I want to understand their level of awareness and respect for people, their emotional stability, and their interest in being in the company of humans. For instance, I know a horse that I would love to coach with. He is intelligent, curious, very interested in being with people, but has one fatal flaw. He is bonded to a mare who lives in the stall next to him. When she leaves the barn he loses it. His attachment to her is so strong that he cannot be relied upon to stay focused on the people he is with and the result is that he could injure someone who is not familiar enough with horse behaviour to notice the signs and anticipate his behaviour.

In order to meet horses where they are, I consider their personal history – as much of it that is known, as well as their current living arrangements. Few horses that live under the care of humans have ideal living arrangements that suit the true nature of the horse. It is my profound hope to one day again be responsible for the care of one or more horses but in the meantime I work with horses that are owned by others. 'Own' is a word I don't care for in relation to living beings, but is the most commonly understood term that humans understand when speaking of animals. I prefer to identify the relationship as one of responsibility – for both parties, me and the horse.

My relationship with any horse I encounter or work with is based on a thoughtful approach to their living conditions, their 'owner's expectations and beliefs about the care of that horse, and my intention to be that horse's reliable respectful consistent leader. I assume responsibility for my communication with the horse and have expectations of the horse that are entirely reasonable and consistent with their abilities and training. I believe the horse also has a responsibility in the relationship: to be prepared to be respectful of humans to the degree that they do not knowingly put people in danger, and that they are able to do the basic things that will be required of them in their lifetime such as respecting peoples' space, standing safely for a farrier or veterinarian, and being willing to load into a truck if and when it is necessary to be moved. These things are, in fact, not just a responsibility but a requirement for a horse to ensure the best chances for success in his lifetime if he lives in the care and control of a human.

When horses live as the property of people and are required to have a job in order to help support the cost of their care, such as farm horses and school horses, it can be tricky to determine if and when a horse is being abused or taken advantage of. In some cases it is easy to see when a horse is being maltreated and there are remedies, albeit weak and difficult to enforce, that can be employed to intervene on behalf of the horse. At other times it is not as cut and dried. Many practices that are clearly abusive and detrimental to the horse are so ingrained in our social traditions that people are blind to them.

Many, but not all, horses have a symbiotic relationship with humans and actually appear to enjoy having a job. When they clearly don't enjoy having that job, are overworked and undernourished, or don't have the time and space to have their social needs met (such as playing with other equines and mowing a lawn for a few hours every day) those horses are living a life that is not natural for them. Unfortunately under today's social and legal rules there is usually no way to intervene on behalf of these animals and provide a more suitable life.

The level of consciousness about horses and animals in

general is in desperate need of being raised. Similar to the way humans have mistreated each other over the millennia, we have mistreated animals. Technology and evolution have brought us to a place today where it is not necessary to continue to do so. According to the Cambridge Declaration on Consciousness of 2012, a cohort of internationally renowned scientists have averred that humans are not the only sentient beings with consciousness and capable of intentionality. Their message is clear - that humans must reconsider their relationship to animals, birds, and some other creatures such as cetaceans and cephalopods. Our cruel and often psychopathic treatment of animals is not justified as it once was thought to be.

One of the most important things I feel I can do for horses that I meet is speak to them in their language. Many horse people claim to be speaking 'equus' but few actually do so with the level of fluency that is possible. Due to the highly evolved ability that horses have to read and understand our energy, horses can and do learn to get along well with well-intentioned humans who speak what I call 'pigeon-horse'. Many people are completely unaware of the language of the horse but who have such a gentle loving demeanor that horses are prepared to overlook any mixed and confusing body language and cooperate for the most part. Some people are sufficiently aware of some of the signals and behaviour of horses to train them to their human version of 'equus'. Conversely, there are many horses who cannot tolerate bad body language. Often these horses develop behavioural problems and may get labelled as problem horses or as dangerous and consequently end up being sent to slaughter.

Speaking Equus

Meeting Comet

As I approach Comet's stall I can tell that he has already spotted me. His reputation precedes him, and has made me all the more curious to 'interview' him. His owner is concerned because his behaviour is problematic: he nips, he pushes into peoples' space, he steps on their feet; he just can't be trusted to be around people and be respectful and polite. He doesn't know how lucky he is; his owner is a woman who cares more about him than his bad behaviour. She hasn't given up on him. She knows that this is the kind of horse that is most vulnerable in this world. These are the ones that can't be trusted to be compliant, that don't seem to respond to standard training methods, the ones that remind you of juvenile delinquents or school yard bullies– the more you try to explain to them why their behaviour has to change, the worse it gets. You set limits and they ignore them. They are the ones headed for jail or in the case of the four-legged bad boys, for the slaughterhouse.

For a horse like this, life will often be a series of sales, being passed from owner to owner, each person using their own brand of horse handling and training, while the horse becomes more and more frustrated and less and less trusting of people. Like a child going from foster home to foster home, the behaviour gets worse as his sense of isolation and self-confidence deteriorate. Trainers who can't figure him out start to tell the owners that the horse is dangerous and ought to be put down. Finally, that is what happens. The horse is picked up by a truck and taken to a feedlot where he will be bought, sold or traded and then sent on to a slaughter house where he will know the agony of a cruel and inhumane death, fully aware and terrified right up until the end.

Comet has his eye on me and, I can sense his strong desire for connection. I do a scan of my physical, energetic, and emotional state and check my readiness to meet this 1,300 pound beast. Thousands of hours of being with and training horses have allowed me to hone a process of mindfully taking note of my inner condition: I start at the ground and feel through my body for any places of physical resistance and check my emotional wellness. I assume the horse I am with will be sensing my energy and clarity of my feelings. It is useful to be as transparent as possible in this moment. Horses are uncomfortable in the presence of emotional and energetic ambiguity.

I find I am ready to meet him. I lengthen my body, standing tall and readying my power centre (the area of your body called the core – the one that Pilates instructors love us to strengthen). His head is hanging over the side of his stall, nodding, and as I come closer he stretches out to try to sniff, nip, push, or lick me. In response, I ignore him, tell him to move away from the door by sending energy to his chest. When he has moved and made room for me I open the stall door. As he moves in to take the space created by the opening I point my dressage whip at his chest, making contact as he starts to crowd me. I tap on his chest. To reinforce and make clear my intention I cluck a couple of times and send energy out from my core to his chest. He stops, nods his head quickly and takes a step backward. I repeat the request and insist he back up and leave me plenty of room to enter the stall. He complies by stepping back a few steps and dropping his head briefly.

Once I am in the stall I stand in the space, claiming it with my energy. I am cycling through my zones of awareness again: my internal state of the eight senses, the appearance of his 'state of mind', and the environment - how much room does he have behind him and on either side, how much room do I have to move in case he charges into me, what other factors are in the environment that might activate his emotional state, how is the flooring, where are the exits, how is he responding to my presence up close.

Comet's head is up and he is eying me, and already deciding that it is time to test the space issue again. This is the most fundamental question for a horse: who pushes who? I quickly respond with consistent gestures - standing tall, sending energy to his chest and telling him wordlessly to stay out of my space. This time I add my hand, holding it out in front of me like a Stop sign as a block that tells him "don't come into this space". At the same time I tap his right shoulder with the dressage whip - lightly at first - asking him to move to his left and exit the stall into his paddock. At first he doesn't respond so I increase the energy intensity with a few more taps of the dressage whip. I am looking for the goldilocks effect – exactly enough energy to convince him that I mean what I say and not a smidgeon more.

He looks me in the eye, drops his head and moves smartly out of the stall and into the paddock. His tail is curled so I know he is not afraid of me. As soon as he is outside he whirls his big body around to face me, curious, even fascinated, and the look in his eyes tells me he is clearly surprised by this unusual human behaviour. I have barely touched him nor let him touch me and boy have I got his attention!

As I step into the paddock Comet is watching me closely. He approaches and I let him come forward until he is about three feet away; then I raise my hand and wordlessly ask him to stop –putting up my hand and engaging my core with blocking energy. He stops and then veers off to my right, making a left turn, showing me his back end as he circles around. As he goes by, I raise my whip just enough to tap his left haunch with a bit of energy and let him know that I know he is being rude and I do not like to be treated rudely. The tap gets his attention and he swings that big rear end around and faces me again. This is the moment where he recognizes I am speaking directly to him – in his language. His head pops up a little bit above level and looks at me with shock apparent on his face, with the whites of his eyes showing. I am not behaving like other two legged creatures he has experienced. I am having a conversation without losing focus, changing the subject, or losing the syntax each minute, nor am I sending mixed messages. I am seeing his responses and hitting the ball back into his court – with relaxed timing, matching his energy, being polite and consistent.

Now he seems entranced and wants more. He starts to approach me again. I swing my core to the left of his head, block his right shoulder with my right hand, point my core to his body and send my whip to his flank telling him to move forward, stay out of my space, and circle around me. As he moves around me I keep my core focused on his body, politely telling him I am to be respected and not to be messed with. His head drops as he moves respectfully off and around me in a circle. When he starts to lose energy and fade to a stop I send him on, widening the circle with signals from my body, making him move on until I can see from his demeanor that he is once again is listening and respecting me.

Like an alpha mare, I want him to know that I am the one to decide how, where, and when he goes. Like an alpha mare, I will tell him when it is OK to stop. When I see he is listening and seems to have gotten the message, I drop my energy, my hands, and I stop sending him on. He comes to a halt, drops his head, licks his lips, and chews softly. We still haven't touched (except for the end of the whip). I tell him what a good man he is a few times and send him heart energy.

I aim my core away from his face and body, hold up my hand to block his head from swinging into me as I approach him, arcing around and toward his body so that I can stand at his shoulder facing in the same direction, shoulder to shoulder. I scratch and run my fingers over his withers, keeping my awareness on his response. As long as his head remains level and doesn't swing into my space, and he doesn't arc his body into me, we are good. We stand together sharing space, a very horse-thing to do. We have made friends. For now.

So what does it mean to speak 'Equus'? This equine language is complex and unnatural for humans. The body language of the horse is very specific but it is possible to communicate with them by using the human body in a way that is recognized by horses as the equivalent of their own movements. Speaking Equus is not an easy thing to learn. Just as it might take years to speak fluent Russian or Chinese, it takes much work and time to become adept at speaking horse to a horse.

In order to speak fluent Equus it is necessary to understand their social structures and needs and to know what priorities horses have. Just as humans have social needs and priorities for shelter, food, and social status, so it is with horses. Differences must be understood though; for example - for a human, shelter is an enclosed space with doors and windows. For horses, enclosed spaces threaten their instincts to flee from danger. In order to live according to the way that suits humans, horses must be desensitized to the small spaces of stalls, trailers, and barns. As social mammals we share the same requirements for the safety we find by living in groups. Living in groups produces in us and horses a set of behaviours that can be complex, involving the need for love and security, the need for access to food and water, and some common understanding of the rules of relating, especially when it comes to sharing food and water, and reproducing and raising young.

"Yet if we look at our evolutionary history, we can see that language is a relatively recent development and was most likely layered upon older signals that communicated dominance, interest, and emotions among humans. Today these ancient patterns of communication still shape how we make decisions and coordinate work among ourselves." (Pentland, 2012)

Millions of years of evolution have moulded the horse physically in ways that are specific to its successful survival. As prey animals who live on four legs, their physical adaptations have produced some very different instincts from us. To start with, horses respond to intention and energy. They do not have the ability to pull so we can communicate on their terms by only moving in the way they move with each other – by push, block and draw.

One doesn't necessarily have to touch a horse to communicate with it. Pointing one's core, our solar plexus, or a finger or a dressage whip, at a horse's sensitive body parts is sufficient to communicate with a horse in order to block a horse's movement or to activate it to move. Horses' heads are highly sensitive to aggressive energy. When you reach for a horse's head to pat it like you would a dog or cat, most often the horse will withdraw its head out of a protective instinct. In order to connect with a horse's head one is more likely to succeed by using drawing energy. My favourite horse trainer Chris Irwin explains this very well in a video on youtube. You can see it here: https://www.youtube.com/watch?v=fq3xCIBcqK8

Horses move in particular ways with each other; they use their heads, shoulders, barrels, and hips to push into each other, to move each other around, and to establish or maintain social order. There are parts of their bodies that act like reflexes such as the "bending button" at the girth line that generates a response for the horse to bend her head towards the towards the source of the pressure (she will usually comply if there is no block to the movement of her head and if she respects the requestor). The part of the body that jockeys hit when they want to make a horse go faster is the soft belly at the flank, unprotected by the ribs and spine, the area that a predator might go after to rip open the horse and take him down. Sending energy to the flank instinctively pushes a horse into more forward motion.

One of the least understood and most fascinating aspects of the horse's body language is the way they relate to spine and girth lines, both with other horses and with humans. For instance, a common training method that may be used to build a horse's confidence can be to allow a scary thing such as a dog or a baby carriage to cross in front of a horse from one side to the other - across its spine line. When the object has crossed this line, a trainer will urge the horse forward towards the scary object. It appears that to a horse, this generates a feeling of confidence that the horse can push the scary thing away. In fact this is also reinforcing an underlying hierarchical notion of who pushes who. Who crosses whose lines is built into this system of jockeying for position. When a scary object crosses a horse's spine and the horse responds by pushing the object away it reinforces to the horse that it is higher in the social order than that thing that was pushed away.

In the normal course of interacting with horses, we miss most of what is going on and when we miss it, we communicate to them that we aren't paying attention or that we are okay being lower in the pecking order than they are. Typically the thing we do most is send mixed messages. Like the experiences I related earlier that brought me to the realization that we are talking to horses all the time when we are with them, I came to understand that developing awareness and being able to be deliberate in my communication with horses was the only congruent and authentic way I could be with them. I have watched more than a few coaches who work with horses unconsciously do things that to a horse would be rude and aggressive while purporting to demonstrate leadership. It is a mixed message at best and an inauthentic example of good leadership to be unaware of the message you are sending. It is a kind of inter-cultural miscommunication that is hard to watch.

The Black Stallion, My Little Pony, or Something In Between

The equine facilitated/assisted learning/coaching/therapy industry is growing. In the last few years the graduates of an ever increasing number of "certification" programs are flooding into a market that is not necessarily developed and ready for coaching with horses. Awareness among the civilian population of this kind of work is spotty and uneven where it exists at all. A concern that I have is that many of these programs require little or no previous horse experience in order to participate and 'graduate'. In this new industry that is springing up where horses are expected to be coaching and healing people, there are no real standards as to the range of experience and knowledge that one needs to have to start a business with horses. The only real laws and governing bodies that apply are the laws related to animal husbandry and animal abuse. Some program developers and leaders are seeking to create standards and accreditation programs which is a step in the right direction. Many people come into the industry out of a love for horses and the desire to "do what you love and the money will follow". Many people claim to understand horses and what they need and how they should be kept and may or may not have enough horse handling experience to actually be competent and responsible for the safety of their clients and the well-being of the horse.

Horses elicit a unique reaction in people that other mammals do not. Most of us have never been up close with a bear or a whale. We don't pretend to know what it would be like to touch them or an elephant or a lion. The inherent uncommonness of these animals generates a curiosity about them. We have no assumptions about how they smell or sound or how they would react to us. The horse however, in its profound familiarity, breeds a different reaction. We take its existence for granted, we are not curious, it is almost as though we don't see them at all because of their reassuring familiarity. Their absence from our daily experience has placed the horse in a unique position in our psyches: that of the very familiar yet rarely encountered foreigner.

Horses are not Disney characters. They have real feelings, real relationships, families of origin, and unique personalities. They have real security needs that are unlike ours and need to be respected for their size and weight. It is my business model to err on the side of caution so I have spent an enormous amount of time and money become knowledgeable about horses, their culture, language, their need for safety and security, and for any needs that may arise for them socially, mentally, and medically.

The model of coaching with horses that I developed is well researched and thought out. My clients will understand that horses do have language and culture. They will know when a horse has just given them the finger or bowed out of respect. Understanding the communication between my clients and the horses is important to the work. My clients do not have to become horse trainers in order to participate but they will understand the basics and know how to communicate to a horse with respect and assertiveness. I have developed my model not based on a theory of how horses are, but on how a particular horse is in relationship with a particular person. To me that makes the experience all the more authentic and magical.

Horse Whispering

Harold was a horse that would not permit a human to kiss his nose or cuddle his head. For whatever reason he never lost his sense of reserve around people. Sometimes when no-one was around and the barn was quiet I would stand next to him, side by side, with my head close to his head, being careful to get only as close as he would allow without moving away. In order to get as close as possible to him while respecting his need for space, I would slow my breathing and get myself into a meditative state. Then I would start whispering to him. I would tell him how handsome he was and how much I loved him. He would always respond by swivelling his ears toward the sound of my voice. He would lower his head and move slightly closer to me, as close as he could without touching. His eyes would soften and close as though he was going to sleep but I could detect that his energy was as active as ever. We would stand like that for several minutes and enjoy the love and joy of each other's company.

Chapter Five - A Model For the Work

"The greatest good you can do for another is not just to share your riches, but to reveal to him his own."
Benjamin Disraeli, 19th century British Prime Minister

Drivers For Change

Coaches are in the change business. Good coaches are in the business of helping their clients to reach for the sky, to extend their grasp - not to grab for what is visible but to imagine the best possible future and create a strategic plan to get there. When we are not reaching for the stars, good coaches are assisting people to look deeply inside and out, identify the change that wants to be born, and to plan and execute on the steps necessary to achieve that change.

Personal and organizational change starts with some motivating factors. In business, change management best practice demands that the organization needs to identify the "burning platform"- the compelling driver for change. When an organization confronts change which involves bringing many minds onto the same page and creating a movement in which most, if not all, parties can buy into the drivers for change, the articulation of a compelling need is an essential starting point. Inertia will otherwise tend to hold organizations and people in stasis.

Coaching engagements for individuals can vary widely from person to person whereas with organizations, planning and delivering on desired outcomes can and must be more of a structured process. There are plenty of well-defined project planning templates that can serve as roadmaps for organizational change. Coaches can accelerate and optimize organizational change when embedded in the work project leaders and organizational change champions. Offering coaching support to those that will be most impacted by change initiatives, or are most resistant, can powerfully shift the odds towards success.

For individuals, I find six to twelve sessions will often suffice to identify and accomplish specific goals; however, manifesting larger visions of change in one's life may need more time. Some people, typically executives, entrepreneurs, and leaders who work in high-pressure situations, like to have a coach on retainer for long-term engagements as a confidential thinking partner.

When coaching individuals, a typical first session is devoted to covering confidentiality, questions and answers about the coaching process, and a full discussion about goals and the context for the coaching engagement. It is also a time that I will start introducing the client to the horse, its language and culture. To be clear, it is not necessary for clients to become fluent in the language of the horse, but it is a transformational experience for people to become aware of the two-way nature of the horse-human relationship. This is a typical outcome of equine coaching sessions.

Typically we will engage in some simple exercises with the horse in each of our sessions. These exercises help to deepen the client's connection to their own internal state – consciously and in particular to the sub-conscious. The second session is typically an exploration into what happened after the first session, as well as a review and a more refined articulation of the goals and vision for the future. Often here we will explore in more depth the client's world-view and beliefs, a further investigation of the present and what wants to change, the known barriers, as well as the identification of resources available to the client, both internal and external. From there, coaching sessions deepen and support the work of the client in moving towards the future state. The role of the horses in this process is to plug the client into their own inner wisdom, intuition, and to generate insight as a direct result of the physicality of being in relationship with the horse.

When working with organizations, more work is required to establish the goals for the group or team. What is it that the leader wants to see change? Typically I will interview each person who will be attending the off-site or retreat and get a sense of the individual goals as well. Equine facilitated coaching is a supportive activity that can be embedded into a change initiative, working with the project team to support the culture change that needs to happen, to deal with resistance, and to help people to embrace the future. For those who will not be part of the future, coaches can be invaluable in supporting people to find a new path forward outside of the organization.

The Domains of the Coaching Journey

Coaches need to be able to work with people and organizations from wherever they are on their journey. People and organizations may start from a ground of questioning with or without clear goals or imperatives, from a place of pain and urgent need for change, or from somewhere in between. In my experience as a coach, the coaching journey can be a direct or winding path that travels quickly or in a more circuitous and lengthy manner towards an opaque or a transparent vision. Often I find, particularly when coaching with horses, that a stated objective can become secondary to another more compelling and urgent issue that arises in a session and a client or organization may want to re-prioritize the goals for the engagement.

The Field of Infinite Possibility

Power	Integration
Clarity	Transformation

Desire For Change

No matter what the issue or issues articulated I see the coaching experience as a flow of experience through four domains that are founded on a platform of curiosity and a desire for change and movement towards an ideal future: clarity, power, transformation, and integration. One can enter these domains from anywhere and move to other domains in any order. In the coaching engagement we live in a world of infinite possibilities. Each client must define for him or herself what that ideal looks like. A coach's role is to support the clarification of the ideal future state and assist the client to make it real by envisioning the path to the future and assisting in identifying and overcoming barriers. There is a notion of an x-y axis in the diagram that leads one to integration but in any coaching journey – and any life journey for the matter - the idea of a destination is illusory. In coaching one enters into a flow of experience. Integration can be a place of arrival that quickly introduces new questions and leads to a need for clarity, power, and more transformation. These domains are not mutually exclusive and can occur in short time frames or occur together without a sense of differentiation.

Clarity

It is pretty easy to get agreement around the idea that clarity is a good thing. Clarity typically is understood to mean lucidity and clear perception. Clarity tends to make things easier - be it personal, interpersonal, professional, or organizational clarity. Coaching for clarity in thought and intention is a natural precursor to clarity in goal-setting and achievement. Typically, speaking aloud our thoughts and questions, our internal dialogues fraught with conflicting assumptions and beliefs, or our greatest fears and loathsome biases, can free us from intellectual dead-ends that we are prone to travel when exploring alone in our minds. Sometime clients have clarity before they come to coaching and have identified the need for a journey into other domains. Sometimes coaching takes place in a state where clarity is not yet present. Getting comfortable with ambiguity and opacity is often a challenge but is a great place to start in a coaching contract where clarity is absent.

I find it sometimes difficult to predict for clients how many sessions will be required to fulfill a client's expressed desires. I have engaged on more than one occasion with clients in as few as three sessions and witnessed a client overjoyed and ecstatic at achieving a coaching goal that he anticipated might take much longer and many more sessions. I also find it difficult to articulate to a client what they will find when they begin an equine facilitated journey. Coaching with horses take us fast and deep into the innermost reaches of the mind, below the level of conscious awareness, and at the same time we delve deeply into the body oftentimes discovering anew - or for the first time - feelings and emotions that are lurking there unattended by the busy data-processing mind.

We each live in a solitary place, our thoughts inexpressible through mere spoken language or even through artistic pursuits. Communication, that concept of exchanging information between parties, is so finite between humans. Our mental capacities, in some ways enormously powerful, are also incredibly limiting and create in us false beliefs and assumptions about the nature of reality. Our busy minds prevent us from experiencing ourselves as integrated beings where mind and body are as one.

My client who I shall call D.H. is a highly intelligent creative who works in a support role in the mental health industry. Her work has a high degree of social complexity and she was working with a very complicated horse when I met her.

"I came to seek knowledge of how to establish physical safe zones when socializing and working with the horse. My inclination to work with horses arose through several desires. Specifically, I choose this work to inquire into a hermetic healing space i.e. one that involved no humans. In the work that I do, I encounter and witness stories of trauma. In the act of witnessing, I sense my own vulnerability. Historically, in the face of this, I've lived through the phenomena of vicarious trauma whereby, my personal history of unresolved, fugitive trauma began to resonate with the others'. The condition of this situation eroded my somatic integrity and my 'somatic ear' no longer differentiated between what was my story and what was the others'. Although I have been in recovery for many years, as I continue to work in the field, it is a vital necessity to also stay in tune with my body. In the presence of the horse, I am delivered into a world of unabridged Beauty. I experience that this presence of pure grace with the horse, empowers me to maintain the balance of my psyche.

After a year of meeting with the horse regularly, I still felt wary. I was having feelings of overwhelm and felt intimidated by the seeming unpredictability of the mood of the horse. [prior to coaching with Evelyn]

While working with Evelyn I began to understand how to communicate with the horse in his language. By applying the principles and the language of the herd, I learned that the horse listened to me by my body signals; and that by communicating and throwing and pointing my chi energy respectfully, I was able to direct him. I noticed that he was happy to be directed, in fact he rewarded me afterwards with soft eyes and affectionate nuzzles.

I gained connection and insight into my interior world of instinct. In order to drop into the subtle language of the herd, the mind must be quiet in order to assimilate this zone. It's a meeting place, a dance; a soft space opens and delivers an awakening to a different centre of consciousness. It's an insight into the field in which I move in the day-to-day at work and where everything can be aggressive. I perceived that a protective armor I carry in front spontaneously begins to recede. What remains is an elastic and fluid feeling. In working with the coach a tri-relational zone arises between Coach, Horse, and Coachee. It forms an insulated space sealed from outside influences, a safe place to explore the interpersonal.

Inquiring into the Equine Facilitated model opened a supplemental world for me to walk in. After performing my role at work, it is not always healthy to seclude to restore energies. However, I am often not up to human company, but I can be alone with the horse - without isolating in my interior world.

Learning ways to truly be safe with the horse translated a certain sense of confidence into my personal life and work life. I can discern what happens within a person when fear and aggression emerge - when boundaries are crossed. What messages am I sending a person with my body and the tone of my voice? How am I physically positioned? Is my body language defusing or blocking?

By working in this way with the horse, the fluid system of my life force opened. These frozen places of trauma melt and recede. I began to discern an instinctual world and my interior responses were reflected by the horse. If I was jumpy and nervous, he would not listen. I learned to be quiet. I entered into unspoken agreements, and by shedding my armor, I saw the horse's personhood and found a playful friend.

The work is meaningful in that it builds knowledge of that space between one and the other. Touching in resonant agreements dropping into/entering a zone containing resonating rapport of embodied communication."

This coaching agreement with this client was a very amorphous one at the start. The client was already enamoured with horses and was somewhat unclear about her goals for the coaching, other than to come into greater communication with a particular horse who was physically challenging. Our coaching touched on shared values, especially her desire to respect the needs of the horse while learning how to keep herself safe.

After the first session, when back at work, she immediately saw how the work translated in her workplace. Learning how to be comfortable with others whose behaviours could be unpredictable and who sometimes challenged her sense of safety was analogous to the work with the horse. Being in an environment where emotional and mental health were an issue contributed to her seeking safety and also raised questions in her mind about how best to assist her clients and not trigger them with her own behaviour, language, and energy. In our second session she related the story of an encounter at work the day following our first session where she was involved with a client whose agitation was escalating. My client intuitively altered her physical stance, in the same way she had done with the horse on the previous day, with the purpose of reducing anxiety and provoking calm. She found her client immediately responded by relaxing and they were able to restore communication in a comfortable way with each other.

In our subsequent sessions D.H. articulated how delighted she was with the clarity she found in understanding her energetic presence and how she could shape it to influence herself and others. Her descriptions of her experiences are uniquely her own and are a powerful testament to the impact that horses can have on us.

Transformation

My client, who I shall call T.C., is a highly intelligent and talented woman who had reached a critical time in her life when she desired personal and professional transformation. T.C. had come through an extremely difficult time of loss on many fronts – financially, with her partner, in her career and with her family. Having worked with and been coached by executive coaches in the workplace, TC was looking for a more profound experience that would galvanize deep growth and be transformational. Our coaching engagement lasted for approximately 18 months and we continue to have tune-up session on occasion.

We worked with a few different horses. In the end, T.C. chose to work with Rocky, a 'been-there, done-that' horse who doesn't suffer fools gladly. This is how T.C. describes the experience:

"I've been doing different versions of Natural Horsemanship for ten years, but knew intuitively that there was something deeper, simpler and more profound in terms of language and technique that I hadn't experienced yet in my connection and communication with horses. When I had the opportunity to take an Equine Coach workshop I jumped at the chance, and I finally found what I was looking for.

I've always loved horses, and have been drawn to them from childhood. At the age of 40 I had the opportunity to be with them, and since then horses are a necessity in my life – like air and being in the sun. Sharing their energy and presence feeds my mind, soul, and being.

The coaching I was looking for was to address not being in my power, finding myself dissociating when in conflict with a (seemingly) more powerful person. I was also working through a lot of grief and trauma that had been unaddressed for many years. In the coaching process I initially was doing what I usually used to do – freezing and dissociating, but then because of the presence of the horse I was working with I realized "oh crap, I have to do something here." I learned from the horses and Evelyn that I could make a different decision, and that I had to move my energy and intention to get out of this stuck place. My resolve was eventually activated, and my energy would flow through and out of me towards Rocky. When I hit this "sweet spot" – I knew that I had it when the physical feeling of "hitting it right" would rise up from my gut and permeate through my body – Rocky would start responding to my request and we began to connect and communicate.

Evelyn provided a safe place to do the work through her calm and obvious expertise. This feeling of being in a "safe container" with Evelyn and Rocky allowed me gradually to overcome the issues I wanted coaching on. I would focus on my goal for the session, and we would do different exercises in the paddock or during walks in Southlands. The experiences generated learning which accumulated both in our sessions and in between.

The learning acted on my subconscious and conscious awareness, and also showed up in unexpected ways in relationships with other people in my life. I was learning true equine communication, identifying and developing the relationship with Rocky by clarifying his boundaries and mine, learning how to ask for different movements, clarifying when he was "playing me" versus when he had a real need for me to be more clear in my communication. I learned how to persist with an "ask" without being rude, getting what I was requesting, and acknowledging him appropriately. All of these lessons translated into how I was in relationship with people, helped me see what I wanted to change, and gave me templates for interacting much more successfully with people.

Evelyn was the leader of the triad: she translated Rocky's behaviour, showed me and then guided me on what to do next from an equine communication perspective. She coached me in the meaning-making process that I was going through, and was essentially an extension of the gifts that Rocky gave me.

Rocky was a sentient partner in my work with him. He

was interested in hanging out with me and connecting and communicating, but first he taught me how to engage with him. He wouldn't respond to my "asks" until I had it all just right – the positioning of my body, the appropriate languaging, and the right amount of welcoming yet firm energy and intention. We would connect and be in 'simpatico' with one another only when I was fully present in myself and calm and clear in my communication. Then we would glide together in harmony.

This approach created an opening for a huge, life-shifting difference. After years of believing that it didn't exist, I now have the ability to find the power center that resides in my gut, invoke that powerful energy so that it expands throughout my body, maintain my equilibrium, and say what I need to say clearly and concisely in difficult conversations. I've learned that I can live in the balance of autonomy, self-determination, power, and grace. I didn't really believe it was possible before working with Evelyn and Rocky."

T.C.'s experience of being coached with a horse as part of the package was, I believe, integral to her finding her own power again. T.C had been living with the results of traumatic life events for so long that she was identifying strongly with her life as being hopeless and impossible to change. For T.C. trying to change her life circumstances has almost become an invitation to be hurt yet again.

As is often the case, when we started our coaching contract I was unaware of the life circumstances that had brought T.C. to this low point. In some respects it didn't really matter. As we worked together with Rocky and focused on how to achieve successes, however seemingly small and insignificant, she slowly began to trust in a future and have hope for a time when she could create the life of her dreams. T.C. is now boldly preparing herself for a new career, is smiling and laughing and enjoying an active social life, and setting appropriate boundaries in relationships that are not serving her. She is almost unrecognizable from the person I first met.

Power

S.T. is a client and coaching colleague who works in the financial services industry. S.T. surprised me, as many clients do, in that she came across to me as someone who, as a successful coach in a tough industry, would appear to be powerful and not feeling inadequate in that realm. Her description of experiencing frustration is a manifestation of feeling a lack of power. Being able to move into the space of allowing things to unfold in their own time is very empowering.

"When I decided to sign up for a workshop Evelyn was doing with horses I was excited and nervous at the same time. Excited, because I wanted to learn something about the horses and leadership; nervous as they had been animals that I had rarely been around and found them big and unpredictable. When I was small my parents put me on a horse with my brother and I wanted off right away. It was too big and went too fast. I had spent some time with Evelyn's horse Harold and found him easy to be around as he didn't seem too gregarious. I didn't get too close and I didn't understand much of what he was doing/saying but was very impressed with how much Evelyn knew about how to communicate with him.

I picked Casey as my horse to work with as she had a bit of a belly and seemed the smallest of the herd. In the round pen Casey was in the corner and I stood in the middle and called her like you would a dog. Casey just stood there. After a while of me calling with nothing happening, I slowly went closer to Casey and for the first time really touched a horse. They are rough and dusty and her skin flinched a lot as I was patting her like a cat. I learned that Casey liked to have a horse pat and I stood by her side and talked for a bit. She was teaching me to build rapport.

I then moved away and tried to get her to follow me. That didn't work and I was getting frustrated so Evelyn suggested I just relax and close my eyes and breathe. Shortly after that my time in the round pen was up and as I stood by the rest of the team to get feedback Casey came over and said "hi" and I patted her on the nose to say thanks. She taught me to relax and know that things will come to me at the right time and I don't need to pull them in; they will come on their own.

Evelyn made the process a safe place for me to learn and experience horses. At one point one of my team members had a horse running around the pen and I looked to Evelyn for safety. She said to stand behind her and I felt much better knowing that she was my protection. Also since Evelyn knows so much more about the horses, I felt comfortable that in each situation she was the expert and I could rely on her to tell me what is going on with the horse. The great part of Evelyn's facilitating my learning is that she didn't take my learning away from me and tell me the answer; she let me try things to see what worked and helped me to understand why things didn't work.

Since my encounter with Casey I am learning that things will come to me in their own timing. I was getting frustrated with clients, prospects, boyfriends who I felt I had to work at getting and was exhausted from all the pulling that I felt I had to do to get them to connect with me. It was like I kept knocking at doors when instead I could learn to answer a door when they knock."

I have continued to coach S.T. on an as-needed basis via

telephone for many months. As the industry in which she specializes changed so did her business and the issue of patience and timing returned for her to wrestle with. In the coaching we did subsequent to the equine facilitated coaching workshop, the feeling and imagery of working with the horse remained as a touchstone and enabled her to become more deeply aware of what was getting in the way of her business. Things turned around dramatically and suddenly for S.T. Finding the inner resources and power that sustained her through an evolutionary period, enabled her to stay positive, focused, and to get clarity on the criteria would need to be true for her vision of success to manifest. And then it did.

Integration

S.A. is a leader, change agent, intuitive, and highly intelligent person who worked in education for many years. When we met she was in a place of wanting to make significant change and plan for the next phase of life. She had a great deal of rich career experience to draw from and, as well as having some exciting visions of a positive future, things were not quite gelling in terms of how to move forward. We agreed to meet for four sessions initially and then re-evaluate her needs at the end of those sessions.

S. had initially been reluctant to participate in equine facilitated coaching despite her deep love for horses. When she finally came for her first session it was a highly emotional experience. What happened for her in that first session opened up some long untouched memories and feelings that tangentially related to horses she had known in her youth. Having a chance to recall those experiences, acknowledge the meaning that she had made of them so many years ago, and come to terms with that part of her past was very significant to her ability to accept the present, move forward, and be ready for the future.

"What stands out for me about the equine facilitated coaching is the gentleness, gentleness from you and from the horse. Acceptance from both as well. A sense of being okay just as I am. It was very pleasant to be in a place where I can just be who I am. In the longer term, the experience left me with a greater sense of self-assurance.

The experience changed me in that I became more confident and self-assured. It helped me move forward with changing my life in new directions. I am applying for new positions and seeking out new opportunities. I am becoming more creative and in charge of my own life. It has been very much a positive change for me. I would say the ROI is quite high."

S. came to our third session having made significant decisions and changes. She said she felt that she didn't need the fourth session but enjoyed it so much she wanted to come back for the experience of being with the horses in the beautiful environment of Southlands in Vancouver.

Teams and Herds

In addition to the one-on-one work, I offer custom off-sites and retreats for groups and teams that want to get out of the office and do something that will have bigger and longer lasting ROI than a golf tournament or a trip to Las Vegas. Working with horses constantly offers analogies to us as to how we are at work with co-workers, customers, clients, and suppliers, up and down the chain of command.

Being out of the office is powerful in the way in which it opens our minds to lateral thinking. The unusual environment

- the smells, sights, and sounds – stimulates our subconscious and conscious thoughts in ways that are highly creative. Being in relation to horses, in addition to each other, offers an interesting interpersonal dynamic that allows people to be more open and intimate in ways that don't happen in the office. In the story below Bob describes standing 'naked' in a ring with a horse as way of creating trust and connection that hadn't previously occurred.

Case study - A High Performing Sales Team

A team from Investors Group, led by a Director who I shall call Bob, came out for a quarterly offsite experience. Working as leaders in the financial services sector each member of the team experiences the stress that goes with managing people in sales positions and meeting consistent performance targets. My experience of the team and their EQ-I reports showed they were a high performing group. Nevertheless, Bob wanted to increase the cohesion and levels of trust among the members.

During the day we had discussions and de-briefs, interspersed with exercises with the horses. Each person had an experience with a horse in the round pen while being coached. The day culminated in a group experience working with one of the horses. It was a true expression of teamwork and they all were very exhilarated by it. I spoke with Bob a year after their one day workshop. I have changed the names to protect confidentiality.

"I was thinking about what we took away from that day and without it sounding too simplistic, I think it was the ability for them to really tap into that feeling component. It was ironic that it took a relationship with a horse for them to have that sense of attachment (to each other).

The example I look to is Jerry's situation. Jerry took the smaller horse, it surprised him how much he felt towards the horse and how much he got back from the horse. That relationship-building exercise for him brought him to a whole different level.

The whole team was very initially supportive about the workshop and the idea behind it although a couple of them were a little apprehensive initially about the horses. Everybody was very impressed with the whole experience right from the initial exercise, the integration of going downstairs and getting a feel for the environment and silently observing the horses, the group work, and the reflection on what happened for each person.

Initially probably within themselves there was an absence of trust. This was an opportunity for them to come together and a chance to stand 'naked' in a ring with a horse that is ten times their size and strength and find a way to battle through their initial fears. They exposed themselves and the team was supportive of it. In the end the group exercise showed how well the team can work together.

They have all gone to different levels within their respective practices. It comes back to their awareness being heightened. No question I have certainly seen changes in Jerry and in Mark I have seen significant changes in Mark in the way he carries himself. In conversation he is more in the moment as opposed to being outside the moment. In a sense he used to pre-judge people and categorize people before they even had a chance. Now he is more receptive to people and allowing things to unfold.

The debrief we had was awesome. After we left you we had another 3 hours of discussion on the ferry and in the car on the way home. We talked about it a lot and it was an important part of the day as a team.

Talking about it now a year later I can feel that the experience is still so vivid for me. One takeaway that still resonates for me is that I try to stay in the moment. I sometimes worry that the team doesn't see all of what I do as the leader in this region. Being vulnerable with the team was the biggest thing for me. Learning more about leadership and not knowing which horse was the alpha, it was interesting that I ended up picking the alpha to work with. It is good to know that inherently the skillset is there. If I stay in the moment I can truly excel in the moment. "

Bob had described his group to me as individuals who performed very well but didn't quite coalesce as a team. He felt they could accomplish more if they relied on each other and operated as a unit instead of as a group of individuals. The workshop offered each person a chance to be alone and vulnerable with a horse in front of their colleagues as well as working together with a common goal of moving a horse through a small obstacle course. The opportunity to be together while doing something unrelated to their normal daily activities in the office, created an awareness in them. By sharing a challenge and seeing themselves and each other in a new and more intimate light they were able to bond in a way that is not possible in the workplace. A year later he described the group as coming together on an emotional level that they had never done before. The subtle yet powerful change that occurred as a result of the time they shared in that one day with the horses surprised him.

Part II

Leadership Lessons from Horses

Chapter Six – The Horse as Subject Matter Expert

"...while we have leadership assessments to... compare leaders to each other, we really have no way of knowing who is a good leader or why. We don't have a theory of what makes someone an effective leader because we don't know what leaders actually do. We can't tell if a leadership development program is effective or not because we don't really know what it does. We can't compare leadership development programs or initiatives. ... You think of some of the challenges we've had is as a society in the last few years and clearly a lot of that is a lack of leadership."

David Rock, Rethinking Leadership, Sept. 2010

Leadership - A Kind of Obscenity?

As I write this chapter, the United States of America is embarking on its lengthy quadrennial march to the polls to elect its ultimate leader. The President of the United States of America, considered by the U.S. to be the "leader of the free world", is arguably the most influential leadership position in the world. Two candidates have been selected by the two major parties and both have historically low approval ratings according to the polls. This leadership campaign is history-making for many reasons not the least of which is the controversial character and anomalous popularity of the Republican candidate.

Despite a plethora of evidence pointing to a high degree of narcissism and egomania, a complete lack of bona fides, and, according to Mark Singer who profiled Trump for the New Yorker magazine, "an existence unmolested by the rumbling of a soul", Donald Trump appears to have a shot at occupying the Oval Office of the White House. (McAdams, 2016) A leadership campaign that has been compared to the rise of Hitler in pre-war Germany appears to have the potential to unseat political policy discourse and replace it with polarizing fanaticism and the cult of personality. Regardless of your political leanings, this race is one for the ages, proof that disruption is not confined to technological change. Debate rages about the cause of this anomalous leadership campaign. Regardless of the cause, it is clear that this debate is deeply rooted in emotion, and emotion it seems is essential to our need and hunger for leadership.

Perhaps leadership today is defined less by the qualities of the leaders and more by the situation in which one finds a leadership void and a public looking to be led. Who will step into the breach, influence the followers, and point the way forward? In the America of 2016, it would seem that the anger and discontent of many of the electorate are sufficiently ignited to generate a firestorm and potentially elect a character who is widely considered to be divisive and mentally and emotionally unsuited to the power of the office he seeks to occupy.

In an era when collaboration and emotional intelligence are touted as essential characteristics for 21st century leadership, we see these notions upended in various political, religious, and corporate arenas all the time. Just as David Rock writes that effective leadership and the evaluation of same, are concepts that are undefined and largely a matter of theory unrelated to the pragmatic instances of real life. It strikes me that the full definition of leadership fails to account for a comprehensive definition of effectiveness and, ultimately, success. Just as one person's trash is another's treasure, one's ideal of leadership is another's inadequate dictator, tyrant or wimp.

In the literature these days there are endless theories and definitions of leadership. A Google search on the term leadership will yield at least 762,000,000 results. There are lists of leadership qualities, books, workshops, and training courses that teach you what kind of leader you are or how to become a leader of this or that type. There are discussions and opinions about whether or not leaders are born or made and if made, how are they made?

Leadership is like obscenity: everyone knows it when they see it but defining it is another story. In the simplest of terms leadership starts with having followers who willingly or unwillingly follow. The corporate and political leader-follower relationship is one that is not unlike an arranged marriage. It is contracted, sometimes directly and sometimes brokered, sometimes desired and sometimes despised. Ultimately leadership must provide a benefit to those who are led otherwise it is not leadership but dictatorship.

The evolution of leadership from ancient times to today, in simplest terms, is a shift from leader as warrior to leader as influencer. True leadership requires a form of consent from followers and history is full of examples of leadership failures resulting in revolution, regime change, and regicide. We live in interesting times, as the Irish curse declares, and are witness to the panoply of political, theocratic, and monarchic types of leadership contracts that have arisen in global societies.

From our Western perspective, especially in politics and business, leadership is largely about influence. Assuming an absence of corruption, leadership is a form of governance where some kind of 'fit' has to be made between the role of leader and the group that follows. Be it through election or selection, leaders are required to provide a semblance of suitability and then, once in the role, meet criteria for ongoing success. In corporate environments, success is typically defined in strategic plans and by financial results. In publicly funded institutions, success is entirely about influence and power as results can be difficult to quantify. In politics, success is the result of the ballot count. None of these is necessarily better than the other as methods for measuring success.

David Rock, the renowned executive coach, author, and co-founder of the Neuro-leadership Institute, posits that we live in the dark ages with respect to leadership and knowing how to increase the measureable effectiveness of leaders. Given the explosion in knowledge available to us today about how the brain works, how groups grow and evolve, the variety and utility of assessment tools - such as emotional intelligence inventories and other psychological instruments, one would think we would be able to improve dramatically the performance and success of our leaders.

Unfortunately, examining leadership by itself will not move us forward unless we view leadership in the context of the whole; we need a systems approach to leadership. We frequently see people selected and put into environments that do not support their success, or the leader's constellation of qualifications and skills is simply not suited to the requirements of the system at the time.

How Leaders Fail

Even when leaders succeed they can be failing the organization. Much has been researched and written about the limiting nature of success with senior executives and leaders. (Chamorro-Premuzic, 2013) Each of us has blind spots. With the most successful executives, danger can arise when success is internalized as though it were a super-power. Hubris, the greatest risk to success, occurs when a leader stops learning and listening to trusted advisors who can provide her/him with invaluable perspective. Relying solely on his or her own ideas and buoyed by the unassailable evidence of past success, there can evolve a culture of sycophants and yes men. Success doesn't tend towards corruption alone but also towards isolation and from isolation it is often difficult for leaders to recover.

I was part of a large organization that had a constantly shifting power dynamic at the senior management table. Over several years a pattern emerged. A vacancy would be created by the involuntary leave of one or more of the senior team. A leader was hired into a vacant position by the most senior leader and a small hiring committee. Within a year the new hire was promoted into a newly created role, custom designed for this newest member of the leadership team; the remaining members of the leadership team were reorganized with new roles and portfolios being changed resulting in resignations and terminations. New openings were created as a result and the pattern would repeat.

The sense of an elitist culture grew up around the senior leader. With every reorganization the feeling of unease and distrust increased in middle management and into the ranks below. Strong capable people resigned or were terminated without a clear understanding of the motivations, the vision, or the direction that the organization was headed. The fallout from that period cascaded throughout the organization having an effect that lasted for many years and manifested as a loss of trust, increased cynicism, a reluctance to speak and act authentically, unwillingness to share honestly with leadership, knowledge hoarding, and an increased level of disengagement among employees. The organization suffered a loss of institutional knowledge, experienced abrupt changes in strategic direction and culture, and was permeated with a sense of a hopelessness as the comings and goings of leaders and key employees continued through a swinging door. The financial cost was significant.

In another situation I was part of a small but rapidly growing business with a single, top-down, leader who held all of the power, affecting the entire organization. This leader was highly distrustful of everyone in the organization while believing himself to be a genuinely caring and sharing person. He described himself as a community builder. The primary motivating force that drove his actions was related to financial and reputational success. He had built an extremely successful organization in a relatively short period of time while, at the same time, losing the support and engagement of his employees. He created employee relations problems that were unknown among his competitors. He was mystified as to why this was occurring and attributed these problems to failures in others, never looking within for the source. He expected his people to be grateful and supportive and could not see that he himself was the source of alienation.

In a third case, a medium sized company undergoing a change in their business model was suffering as a result of a loss of faith and trust between the partners. Feelings were so strong and communication so lacking that the partners could not meet fact-to-face. In the void created by the absence of firm visible leadership there was a jockeying for power that had a palpably destructive effect on relationships within the company and threatened its future. It was only when the partners were willing to repair their relationship that they were able to begin to define the strategic planning necessary to move the company forward. Meanwhile the impact of several years of a dysfunctional leadership team had an adverse effect on the company's culture and bottom line.

Many years ago a friend was hired into a senior leadership role by one of Silicon Valley's greatest companies in its earliest days. My friend was head-hunted away from a very prestigious position in a large well-known and very successful company on the East Coast. The opportunity looked like a dream job. Silicon Valley was not yet on everyone's lips as the hub of America's new economy but insiders knew the future was in the digital age and Silicon Valley would be leading the way into the future.

After an intensive selection process my friend was offered a premium job and of course, grabbed the chance. Within six months it was apparent to both my friend and the leadership of the new company that things were not going to work out. What had appeared to be a spectacular career in the making began to look more like a career disaster. In the discussions about how to manage a reasonable and fair transition from the company HR offered to do a personality profile to assist in a successful relocation for my friend. What was discovered was that my friend and his boss were polar opposites in personality type – a nightmare pairing that without careful coaching was bound to end in conflict and misunderstanding. I was struck by how unfortunate and costly a mistake it was not to include the assessment in the selection process. How often do we see wrongful hiring lead to a wasteful dismissal.

In each of these stories there is a litany of missed opportunities and a certain amount of hubris. In all cases there is a cultural, emotional, and/or intellectual mismatch between leadership and the corporate ranks or a mismatch within the leadership ranks. Business success is not determined only by the education, experience, and cultural fit of individuals alone but also by the psychically and emotionally primitive beings we are.

Emotional intelligence, neuroscience, and executive coaching have a great contribution to make in the workplace to reduce the expensive and inadequate "complete guesswork" that David Rock describes in his article. In addition to the benefits that can be derived from these progressive disciplines, experiential learning and equine facilitated coaching has much to offer. The learning that is possible when one is engaged with non-verbal sentient beings is powerful. The combination of reflective introspection, receiving the unfiltered individual feedback from horses enhanced by experiencing the emotional and physiological components - not just the intellectual, creates the ideal conditions for deep personal and organizational change.

Embodied Leadership in Action

I was really late. I had taken a scenic backroad route. The day turned out to be less than ideal as a wild sudden squall swarmed over the mountains and raged up the valley, bringing what felt like hurricane force winds and driving rain sideways into the windshield of my car. I heard a shocking thunderclap and looked ahead to see a power pole swing erratically over the country road. The powerline snapped like a bull whip and snaked towards my car landing directly in front of me. Seeing it coming I braked and managed to stop short just in time.

I was on my way home to Vancouver after visiting family and friends in Calgary Alberta. I had planned to stop in Kamloops, British Columbia to audit a clinic with my horse training guru Chris Irwin and now it looked like I was going to miss the whole morning. This was before the days of GPS but I was lucky; I doubled back and took a gamble on another mountain back road.

I arrived at the clinic in time to see Chris start working in the round pen with a very flashy young Arabian pony. They were facing each other, the horse looking around coolly, sussing out the whole arena, obviously a very intelligent animal and not the least bit nervous about finding himself in new surroundings. His name was Fire and, as it turned out, it was a perfect fit for his temperament.

Fire had come down from a ranch near Prince George, British Columbia. In his limited world view and life experience he likely believed himself to be pretty darn special and near or at the top of the herd hierarchy. The way he moved and looked us all over told us that he was not afraid of anything and ready for everything.

Chris raised his lunge whip to level and gently and firmly touched the horse on his left front shoulder, asking him respectfully in equine body language to move over. Like the storm I had just escaped and in the blink of an eye, the Arabian was up on his hind legs, hopping forward towards Chris, snapping his jaws like an alligator and stabbing the air with his front hooves. I had never seen such aggression in a horse before and I am certain my jaw fell open, as did all of the other human jaws in the arena.

As always Chris did the smart thing: he quickly got out

of the round pen and started working with the horse from outside the pen. I watched in awe as he deftly 'talked' with the horse, in the horse's language, matching each and every lift and swish of the tail, arch of the neck, swing of the butt, with a lift and swish of the whip, calmly, firmly, and consistently seeing every move however small or fast, answering every challenge with a clear consistent demand for respect. Soon Chris was back in the round pen and over the course of the next 20 minutes, I watched an unbelievable transformation. Fire began walking politely and calmly alongside Chris, head low, licking and chewing, and giving Chris the respect and deference that was due a true leader who had proven his worth.

All this had occurred without dominating, bullying, or beating the horse but instead by speaking to the horse in the language he understood while maintaining respect and some amazing physical athleticism on Chris' part. By demonstrating to Fire that Chris possessed the level of awareness and ability to speak Equus, the horse was willing to trust Chris to be with him and accept him as his leader.

Chris Irwin describes what many horse people know to be true about the magic of working with horses. "Every moment you're with them, they're taking your measure with the accuracy of a creature whose very survival depends on precise readings of its environment. You can't fake it with horses. You'll just confuse them and frustrate yourself if you try. …you must open your mind and allow your horse to show you how to communicate with the same depth and transparency it has. And that's when the magic starts."

The magic that Chris describes is where the power of equine facilitated coaching lies. Chris describes the demand that horses have of us to "be our best selves". The requirement to look inside for the source of any miscue, disturbance or undesired result is what creates in us the kind of discipline that builds better leaders- the ability to own your sh*t.

Fire. Photograph reproduced with permission by the photographer,
D. Henckel

The Horse as Leadership SME

SME, pronounced 'smee', is an acronym for Subject Matter
Expert, a term used to denote authority and expertise in a topic.
I refer to the horse as a leadership SME because they spend
most, if not all, of their time testing each other's leadership
capabilities. We think this sparring and play-fighting serves
two purposes from a survival perspective: it trains the horse to
maintain constant alertness and it tests the fitness of each animal
to be a leader if and when a predator appears. The added benefit
from this interaction is that it creates, builds and reinforces the
social bonds that knit a herd together. On a moment-to-moment
basis each horse wants and needs to know where he or she is
in the herd hierarchy. Every new day is a good time to check
for any loss of strength or leadership credentials. Every new day
or change to the makeup of the herd is an opportunity for a
leadership convention and possible regime·change.

Horses are mammals like us but, as prey animals, their survival strategies are different from ours and other predators. Like the zebra, horses evolved to live on the plains, grazing and browsing, continuously moving to where food and water are in suitable supply. The horse's primary strategies for surviving its predators are to see them well before they are close enough to strike and to be able to outrun them. Horses do not seek out caves, build dens and burrows, or have anything that resembles our version of the safety and security of a home. Horses naturally desire open spaces so that they can avoid becoming trapped. Like other social mammals, they seek to live in groups. Having membership in a herd increases your survival odds by sharing the duties of watching for predators, finding food and water, being able to sleep while others are on watch for danger, and looking after the young.

Alpha-mares and Alpha-stallions. Who is in Charge of Who?

For many years the assumption about the nature of the equine herd was that a stallion had a harem of mares that were his. He made all the decisions, fought off all invading competitors, and the mares followed him and willingly had his offspring. The truth turns out to be quite different but I find it very interesting that upon casual observation of horses in the wild, it was possible to miss the true nature of the social structure of horses. It is a testament to our observational powers to miss significant information because of our assumptions. In the case of the equine herd, the male dominated social model appears to have influenced the vision of the equine herd (Williams, October 2015).

In fact research has shown that the herd is matriarchal

with the stallion acting more as bodyguard. While he is indeed fighting off competitors, apparently he doesn't have exclusive breeding rights. It has been shown that mares will sometimes prefer other stallions and leave a herd to mate, sometimes returning and sometimes staying with other preferred mates. Alpha mares will control the movement of the herd and the access to resources. She will determine who gets water first and last and which gets the best grass. Males that are superfluous to the breeding requirements of the herd are ejected when they are old enough to survive successfully and will join a bachelor herd where leadership is sorted out on a daily basis. These bachelors will attempt to take the place of breeding stallions throughout his life. His fitness to lead is under constant performance review. Mares will often employ cooperation and collaboration strategies to get their way or to maintain stability in a herd.

A model of equine leadership described by Carolyn Resnick, a renowned equine trainer, divides horses into 3 groups: leaders, dominants, and followers. Leaders in the herd are often mistaken as omegas or followers as they do not exhibit competitive behaviours, often spend their time physically at a distance from the rest of the herd, and do not display signs of paying attention to other herd mates – when in fact they are paying keen attention. Followers are easy to confuse with leaders although they may be more likely to be physically closer to herd mates. Most horses fall into the middle group – dominants, displaying competitive behaviours that could be mistaken for leadership. These horses are vying for position; they don't want to be last to eat and drink and want to be as close to the top of the hierarchy as their fitness permits. This is a survival strategy that has enabled horses to succeed as a species for over 40 million years. This model fits the human model of leadership as well. It is easy to see those jockeying for position as "wannabe" leaders. The leaders we usually respect the most are those that we naturally are drawn to respect and trust.

Aside from the three groups defined above, we believe that all members of the herd support a distributed model of supportive leadership in the herd. Horses hold a place of leadership specific to their abilities and to the needs of the herd over time. The alpha mare or stallion (the leaders) have overall leadership responsibilities for the herd but some jobs are delegated. Research has shown that some horses will act as pacifiers and assist horses to "kiss and make up" after disputes. Some act as caregivers, looking out for foals, the injured, or elders. Some will enforce discipline even on higher ranking members for the betterment of the herd.

Equine leadership is worn like a mantle without any outward behaviour manifested other than a demeanor that is calm and non-reactive. The leader of the herd is usually a mare and the work of keeping the herd together is delegated invisibly to her lieutenants. They are the ones who enforce order, start and end fights, and compete for status within the group. The alpha has only to look at her lieutenants to send a clear signal of discipline. In fact it would appear that alphas only tell herd mates what not to do by the subtlest of signs such as a look, a pinning of ears, a swing of the hips, or a step in the direction of a horse who may be causing offense. The worst thing that could happen to a horse is to be ejected from the herd so the motivation to comply is strong. Resnick believes that the true leader is one who is 'liked' by all or most of the herd members. It would appear that at the very least, the herd trusts the alpha implicitly – until they don't. Then a leadership review is in order.

Research also shows that the alpha mare isn't necessarily

the horse that the rest of the herd follows in times of flight from danger. In fact the roles that are fulfilled in a herd of horses are often shared out of necessity and presumably aid in the knitting together of the family or herd structure. Mares will share the duties of rearing and protecting foals. All the members of the herd share in the duties of protecting each other during periods of rest and sleep. One will rarely see a whole herd lying down; one, at least, of the herd needs to be seen to be standing guard.

The stallion plays a significant role in the protection of the herd because in the wild, stallions will try to steal mares. Stallions without a 'harem' live out their lives in bachelor bands, herding together for protection from predators but unable to mate unless they can conquer an aging or otherwise less fit competitor. The competition among horses then would seem to be prevalent but it is not directly for resources, it is for position.

Not much is known about leadership and horses due, in part, to the difficulty of studying horses in a natural state. Up until recently, there was a low level of interest in the study of either the horse as livestock or the horse as a feral animal. (Horses do not exist today as truly wild species. They were hunted to extinction in the wild and survive as livestock or descendants of domestic stock.) Horses that are domesticated are difficult to study for norms as they live mostly in unnatural conditions of captivity and confinement with highly controlled breeding restrictions.

What is clear from observation of horses is that horses rely on their leaders and herd mates for a sense of security and order. Group cohesion is important and a change in the make-up of a herd will result in unease and an upsurge in competitive behaviours until the pecking order is clarified.

The Horse Human Comparison

"Indeed, long-term observation of these animals in the wild is like following a soap opera. There is a constant undercurrent of arguing, of jockeying for position and power, of battling over personal space, of loyalty and betrayal."
Wendy Williams, 2015

There is much in the social structure of horses that is insightful and instructive for us humans. Humans, having a neocortex and neurological mechanisms that enable us to evaluate emotional input and respond in an appropriate and measured way, have an advantage that horses do not have.

Or do they? The evolution of the human brain has produced in us a greater level of social complexity and an ability to be disconnected from our emotional selves. As Shakespeare said "There is nothing either good or bad, but thinking makes it so".

In our human societies, leaders do not have a defined constellation of characteristics. Leadership characteristics and power dynamics are more complicated in human herds than in equine herds. Over thousands of years, leaders have generally evolved to become less like warriors, or alpha stallions, such as Alexander the Great or Ghengis Khan. They are more like icons whose power source emanates from wealth and/or charisma, and who are more intelligent and skilled at presentation and persuasion. In this evolution away from warrior based leadership to persuasion, influence, or wealth based leadership, we see increased complexity in the management of power and the role of influence.

Consider some of notable leaders of the past and present: Abraham Lincoln, Mao Zedong, Catherine the Great, Idi Amin, Barack Obama, Adolph Hitler, Winston Churchill,

Engele Merkel. Each of these historically important leaders has had supporters and detractors; each made huge contributions, positive or negative, to the viability and success of their countries; each had a role to play in the deaths of thousands of people; each changed the history of the world in some significant way. Some are regarded as heroes; some are seen as traitorous manipulative dictators. Your view of these historical giants will be shaped in part by the culture and context in which you live and less by the leadership qualities of the individuals.

Leadership is not just about education, experience, and skill. It is also about context. We humans compete for dominance in much the same way as horses and other mammals however we are less conscious of the signs and symbols of competition.

"...which animal the ruler should impersonate depends strongly on what animals the followers are."
Geert Hofstede, Cultures and Organizations: Software of the Mind (Hofstede, 2010)

I maintain my credentials in horse training by participating every year in clinics with my mentor and teacher Chris Irwin as well as volunteering part-time to retrain off the track thoroughbreds (known as OTTBs) so that they can be placed with a rider and have another career once they leave the racing business. Thoroughbreds are highly observant and responsive horses. I call them hair-trigger horses because they are so responsive to the slightest signals and energy levels. Like people, horses are all different. What works for one horse may very well not work for another. I had an experience working with one thoroughbred that was very instructive.

We went into the round pen, Charlie and I, and the game started when Charlie ignored my boundaries and request for respect by stepping forward boldly when I asked him to back up by touching his chest with my dressage whip. Game on! As I pushed the horse (energetically), asking him to move out to the edge of the round pen and be respectful, I was able to get to a level of respectful response from him but couldn't get him to consistently show me respect. He was changing direction, turning respectfully head in to me about half of the time and the rest of the time rudely turning his back-end in to me. We worked at this for about 10 minutes, me asking Charlie to turn, him giving me about 50% respect. Chris, my mentor, watched and finally he stopped me and asked me to straighten my spine and push my chest out a little, literally to stand taller. As soon as I physically altered my stance and my body language the horse changed. Suddenly I was worth taking seriously. Suddenly I was getting the respect that I couldn't get in the previous ten minutes. Every turn I asked for I got with respect - Charlie carefully turning in to me with his head instead of with his rear end. The miniscule physical difference of straightening my spine changed Charlie's perception of me and suddenly I had some 'cred'.

Interestingly, as has been pointed out in studies related to power and body language, the change in my physical presence changed my own emotional state as well. I believed in myself more and the belief was reinforced by the horse's behaviour. Amy Cuddy has done valuable research on the effects of our body language in terms of the poses we take and how they affect ourselves and others. Although she didn't mention horses, they are at least as keenly observant and susceptible to the same kinds of cues as humans.

This combination of hyper-awareness and responsiveness is probably the most important set of qualifications that allows a horse to trust and accept a leader.

Bespoke Leadership

Leadership that accounts for context as well as the needs of the followers might be called custom or bespoke leadership (Martin, 2014). The idea that character, skills, and education are insufficient to ensure an effective leadership match should not be foreign but often is. The idea that the needs of the followers and the context in which the organization finds itself, ought to be factored into the choice of leaders, might go a long way to closing the gap to which David Rock refers.

In any context where leadership is at issue and organizational change is required, we ought to be asking questions such as:

- What are the vision, mission, goals of the organization and how clearly does the whole organization understand them?
- Who supports these ideas and why?
- Who is undermining these ideas and why?
- How seamless is the cascade of governance in the organization?
- How strong is the culture and what resistance or support for the leader can be anticipated based on the culture?
- What are the motives of the leaders and leader candidates? Are they interested more in power, their own careers, and compensation, than in the well-being of the organization?
- How engaged are the followers? What does it take to have a followership that is engaged?
- What obstacles are in the way of progress towards group unity?

- What resources are available to support forward progress?
- How will we measure success?
- How long is the term of leadership and what will be the leader's legacy?

Bespoke leadership implies that leaders can be placed in situations that best serve the needs of the organization at times when the qualifications will be the most effective for the greatest good of the organization.

Leadership Lessons from Horses

I have learned many leadership lessons from horses. Once I came to understand their need for leadership and their near-obsession with it, I began to let go of the idea that we were 'partners' and potential 'friends'. Just as you can't truly be only a friend to your children – you need to be consistently a parent too - so we need to accept the responsibility for the welfare of horses and the requirements they have that allow them to thrive. Similar to the way I have felt reluctant as a leader of people, I was reluctant to take a leadership role with horses until I understood their deep need for it. In fact, understanding this need allowed me to accept the role of leader in the workplace with more ease.

Lesson #1 – Respect Before Trust; Trust Before Love

When we meet someone new we begin to form a relationship based on first impressions and then the relationship will evolve based on experience. The anatomy of relationships and how they form and evolve is a complex interweaving of physiology and psychology that has a significant unconscious component. With horses as with people, respect, trust, and love are requirements for positive relationships.

The leader who remembers names of spouses and children is one who is paying attention and, more importantly, who is perceived to be paying attention. The power of a leader's attention and awareness cannot be overstated.

Psychologists tell us that in our daily interactions we unconsciously train people to treat us the way they do. It's the Golden Rule in action but not the way we usually think of it. Are there relationships you have at work where you feel you are not getting the respect you would like and feel you deserve? Are you demeaned in ways that make you think you are not being taken seriously? Conversely, is there someone who maintains a distance and gives the impression they might actually be intimidated by you? What signals are you picking up? How can you test the reality of these impressions? What might you be doing to create these imbalances in relationship?

It is common at home and in the workplace for these kinds of undercurrents to show up at times with some of our friends and colleagues. When it isn't a problem we tend to let these things slide, often because we don't know how to deal with them. We don't know where to start.

These undercurrents became much clearer for me through working with horses. Horses are pretty pragmatic in their relationships. They are constantly interacting and often playfully sparring. Horses left to play together in pastures will spend a certain amount of time provoking each other and playing 'king of the castle' games. In fact they are playing games that are essential to their survival. They are 'awareness' games. To be unaware is to risk injury or death.

It is typical for people who come to be coached with horses to be most concerned initially about whether or not the horse likes them or knows that they are feeling fearful. In my experience, it takes some time for a horse to decide if he or she likes you or not. Typically what the horse wants to know is can they respect you and if the answer to that is yes, then the next questions will be can they trust you. To be clear, respect like trust, has to be earned and both take time.

Horses are pragmatic about respect, trust and love. With horses respect has to come before trust. Without respect trust is just not possible. Once respect is earned (and maintained) then the trust can start to grow. Eventually love may also grow. Where love flourishes, respect and trust also flourish.

The language of equus is a very physical and precise language. Horses have a specialized physiology that has defined their survival and their communication strategies. They have eyes on the sides of their heads which enables almost 350 degree vision, most monocular and some binocular. This, plus the underdeveloped corpus callosum, likely helps to account for the fact that they seem to require training on both sides of their bodies. In fact it is common for a horse to see something with one eye while travelling in one direction, and when seeing it with the other eye while moving in the opposite direction be startled by the object.

Not having opposable thumbs, and because they structurally load about two thirds of their body weight onto their front legs, horses cannot pull. They move around and with each other by pushing, blocking, and drawing, both energetically and physically. If you watch horses playing together you will see this way of interacting quite clearly. Horses will push each other away from food or water without making contact, sometimes simply by moving in another's direction, sometimes by adding additional cues such as pinning ears, biting or turning and threatening with a kick. Often a horse will stand between a horse and the water or hay feeder. This blocking is a display of hierarchy and may be an invitation to play leadership games. Drawing energy is subtle and often unnoticed. Horses draw with their bodies by the way they arc away from another horse or human, or by a lowering of the head.

Since coaching with horses I have found most people have some confusion about the differences between respect, trust and love. Working with horses is a powerful way to get clarity around these important relationship fundamentals.

Lesson #2 – I Am Responsible for my Results.

The solitary experience of riding and learning to groom and care for horses was where I was coming up against my own assumptions, beliefs, prejudices, and personal failures. I often wanted to project my inability to make the horse do what I wanted onto the horse. My instructors wisely insisted that the horse was not in any way responsible for my lack of ability or failure in communication skills. Slowly it was dawning on me that I was being taught leadership in a completely new and radically different way.

My inner awareness increased dramatically the more I spent time with the horses and I was seeing myself in stark black and white perhaps for the first time in my life. As I learned to take responsibility for my actions, all my actions, regardless of my skills and aptitudes, I started to experience a sense of compassion for myself much like I was experiencing for the horses. Previously, very much a loner, I had believed that we are each responsible only for ourselves and our own feelings. Now I started to experience the grey areas and understand that consideration for others' feelings, waiting for others to catch up, or helping others get to the same place as you was not a sign of co-dependence. Where I would previously shun help from others and prized my independence, I now realized that there are good reasons to join the herd.

Etiquette in the riding ring mimics etiquette in other areas of life and yet again I was learning simple lessons from the horses. In the winter it was common to be riding indoors with as many as six or seven other riders. That adds up to twelve or fourteen beings in a relatively small space. When one horse would bolt and start to gallop in the arena the other riders would stop and wait for the rider to get her mount back under control. The first few times it happened I was taken aback. My expectation was that it was the rider's responsibility to sort her horse out and I could carry on doing what I came to do. I came to realize that riders were concerned not about their own agenda but about the well-being of all the horses and people in the ring. The one horse that was bolting was experiencing fear and stress and the other horses were sharing those feelings. The riders, more experienced than I, were doing the most considerate and appropriate thing from a safety and relationship perspective. They were demonstrating their caring for the feelings and safety of themselves and each other and I began to see that my over-valuing of my independence could have a down side that I previously had not considered.

When I started riding lessons I was scatter-brained. My attention seemed like it was everywhere at once. Keeping my heels down. Sitting up straight. Dropping my shoulders. Relaxing my arms. Not pulling on the reins. Keeping my heels down. Wondering what that twitch of the horse's ear meant. Why is he stopping? Dropping my shoulders. Lord my thighs hurt. Why is he speeding up? Sitting up straight. etc. I think you get the picture. I thought I would be stuck in the space of conscious incompetence forever.

It became apparent fairly quickly that horses had some say in the matter of whether or not to go forward or to stop if I asked. They were not like motorcycles where you turned a key, put it into gear, and give it some gas. I could be turning the key and following all the instructions to go forward and my horse would stand on his feet completely and literally 'unmoved' by my desire. It appeared that although school horses are trained to be gentle and let people learn how to ride they are still not without opinions.

At some point early in my student rider career, the fact that horses had their own opinions initially led me to think that I could blame my inadequacy on them. I did squeeze my legs and cluck and yet he didn't walk on. Not my fault – stupid horse being recalcitrant/not listening/being stubborn. None of my many instructors accepted that premise for a nano-second. In fact they made it clear it was ALWAYS about how I asked the horse. Blaming the horse was simply not allowed. Eventually I learned that getting a horse to go forward was not only about the right body cues; it was also about what was going on inside of me. I had to learn to align my internal states with my desire to move forward, come to a halt, go from walk to trot, and back to a halt. Again, this business of inner awareness was always at play and I always had to take responsibility for my inner and outer physical, emotional, and intellectual states.

I thought about that a lot over the weeks, months and years of learning to ride and the mulling of this lesson carried over into the office while managing people and carrying out my duties under a variety of difficult and often highly stressful conditions. Every time I found myself wanting to excuse myself for not making the grade by making it someone else's fault, I knew deep down that that was the easy way out and was neither true nor useful. It is always about my part in the relationship. I create the results in my life and when I remember that, I have the power to change things that otherwise would be impossible to change.

Lesson #3 – I Saw That

Did I mention that awareness is everything? Horses are the masters of awareness but humans also have powers of awareness and often we do not pay attention to the information we are collecting through our many senses. This is because we are cogitating, in the default mode brain network, and our focus is in the past and the future. Our brains are collecting data in the present; we know this because we can recall it later but in the moment we are often not actually living in the moment.

When working with horses, one of the most effective strategies that can make a difference and up the level of respect is to tell a horse you notice when he is doing something disrespectful. One of a myriad of ways in which a horse will test awareness and check your leadership credentials, is to move into your space forcing you to take a step backwards. Horses do this a lot and it is common for people not to see it and to take a step backwards without thinking. By not seeing this little tidbit of communication people give the horse the idea that they are indeed less worthy or lower in the pecking order than the horse. Seeing these little tests of awareness and respect and responding to them by telling the horse not to take your space – effectively saying "I saw that and it's not OK" - is a powerful way to start getting respect from a horse.

The same can be said for human to human relationships. We train people every moment in how to treat us in exactly the same way we train a horse or a dog. When we are unaware of the smallest non-verbal and verbal cues that speak of disrespect, or when we notice them but do not respond to them, we create the potential for miscommunication or unpleasant behaviours to occur. When a horse disrespects us there is some potential risk; it can result in crushed toes or worse. With people the unfortunate results may not be physical but there are likely to be repercussions.

Coaching with horses around this topic is very powerful. Once people notice when a horse is dissing them it becomes a powerful way to look at the results we are getting in our lives around respect. Simple interactions with horses that highlight this for clients is like putting flood lights on a problem. Becoming conscious and aware in the moment when we are letting people disrespect us or see us without power is life changing. Coaching people around this topic can create positive major changes in one's life.

Lesson #4 – Goldilocks and Emotional Intelligence

Prey animals do not want to show vulnerability. Showing vulnerability is an invitation to predators. Like a horse I was raised to hide my feelings. Many of us are and perhaps this stems from the same instinct. In adulthood I was told I ought to express myself more openly, that expressing your feelings was healthy and letting other people know what was really going on was better than bottling things up and confusing people.

To a great degree this is true. Learning how to express yourself at the right time, in the right place, with the right person, in the right way - especially at work, is the domain of emotional intelligence. As an adult I undertook to find good role models – leaders – that I could emulate. In fact I found both good and bad leaders were great role models. In the early years of my career I learned through trial and error. Over the years as a leader, finding myself in increasingly demanding situations that taxed my abilities as an emotionally competent leader, I can honestly say I did the best I could at the time. Had I the chance to do it again, I would prioritize developing greater emotional intelligence sooner in my career.

I rarely felt confident in the workplace. I always felt a niggling sense of anxiety that I wasn't doing leadership well enough, that there were better ways if only I could think of them. I am an introvert and was a sufferer from the Imposter Syndrome. I learned finally that I could not be the judge of how well I was doing. I learned I had to let go of thinking about my performance and pay more attention to my gut and do a checklist of things to evaluate my performance. I could never control how others would perceive my value and worth in the workplace. I had to turn it over and let the universe take care of me. As long as I was doing what I considered to be the best I knew how, then it was no longer my business to second guess what others thought.

Most of this I learned in the time I spent with horses. Spending hours every week in the Sphere of Awareness helped to develop my skills of self-awareness, emotional self-management, enhanced my ability to manage stressful demands in the workplace, and improved my relationships in and out of the office.

Lesson #5 – The Grass Is Greenest Right Under My Nose

For a horse the grass is greenest right under your nose. If I had a dollar for every time I took a horse for a grass walk and watched him aim for the closest blades while I spied Much Greener Much Better Grass a few feet away I would be a millionaire. Horses do not see grass the same way I see grass. First of all they don't just use their eyes. They definitely use their noses and, if it passes as edible, they will eat it no matter how short, sparse, or pale it appears to me. I have tried to tell them the grass is greener somewhere else on many occasions and they don't seem to care. They live in the moment dealing with what is in front of them.

This notion has many lessons embedded in it for me. Being a human as I am I have a tendency to live in the future and the past where I have many examples to compare this grass to better grass I have seen before or hope to see again. I can become embroiled easily in strategizing about how to find and secure better grass so that I will always have a good supply. I can be so wrapped up in the memory of better grass or the anticipation of great grass in the future, that I can really judge the grass in front of me as unappealing and not really worth the effort. I can have the grass in front of me and not really be aware of it because I am so caught up in the idea of where better grass can be found.

Horses are the best teachers of mindfulness that I know. If nothing else, the greatest skill I have learned from spending time in the presence of horses is who to live more fully and completely in the now.

Lesson #6 – Know When To Be Flexible With The Agenda

As a manager with many active projects, competing priorities, and a large number of staff I tended to be fairly directive with people and driven by deadlines. I was told many times in my life that I was my own worst enemy, that I am stubborn, and I know I was a perfectionist. For most of my career I was very task focused and it was only through my work with horses that I came to reflect and understand why being relationship focused was likely a more winning strategy in the long run. Being task focused meant sticking to the agenda, the timelines, and the deliverables unless there were compelling reasons to change. Eventually the horses got through to me and I could see more often that sticking to the agenda wasn't always the best course of action. I started to learn to read the signs and re-evaluate priorities more often when signs and signals gave me pause to reconsider. The following was one of the first times that a horse got me thinking about my agenda and whether or not I needed to recalibrate.

It was a perfect day to take Harold to the club. After two months of rehabilitation he was ready to be trotting up to fifteen minutes with a break and then another fifteen minutes. I was told once that sports medicine was invented at the race track rehabilitating race horses. The similarities are there; thoroughbreds are athletes and getting an injured horse back in shape to continue its racing career is handled very much like a human athlete's rehabilitation.

Harold was a very respectful and reasonable horse. I had been riding him for a couple of years. He had never bolted, bucked, or thrown a rider to my knowledge so I had no concerns about him from a safety perspective. This was my first experience rehabbing a horse though and I was unused to some of the psychological behaviours that can arise in a horse that has been injured.

The area where Harold boarded was near to a riding club, a

fabulous facility that had a number of riding rings for different riding disciplines as well as a track for cantering. I felt taking Harold to the club was the perfect way to start getting him ready to go back to work. He was still a school horse at this time. He needed to get back in shape so he could be used as a lesson horse a few days a week.

Because he had been off for several months he hadn't had his shoes put back on yet so I walked him the three blocks to the club to save the wear on his hooves. I was going to mount him at the club, have a workout and then walk him home again.

As we walked I could feel the tension building in him the closer we got to the club. I was a little surprised as he was used to going to the club, it was a lovely day, and there were no distractions that might get a horse worried and feeling unsafe. I was still relatively new to the horse training method I was learning from Chris Irwin but I had all the confidence in the world that I could handle Harold – until we got onto the club property that is.

As we walked down the track towards the mounting block Harold got out of hand, literally. He started pulling and prancing and acting like a crazy horse. I knew enough to try and keep his head level or low and circle him to expend the adrenalin that was coursing through his body. Circling helped to get his focus back briefly but as soon as I came out of the circle and started towards the mounting block again he started acting up. Next thing I knew he was rearing. Now I was scared. I had never tried to hold a horse under these conditions. The sweet mild-mannered Harold I had known had suddenly turned into a wild mustang. Other riders on the track looked askance as they tried to pass us without having the fear spread to their own horses.

I was committed to not using dominance to get him to

behave; other riders would simply have sharply yanked his reins and used the crop to strike him. Instead I continued to work on keeping his head level and circling him to permit the adrenaline to run its course. Eventually I realized that I was not going to be able to calm him down. He did not want to be at the club that day! It took what felt like days but was probably only an hour to slowly circle him and work him back towards the exit gate. By then of course I was as tense as he was. As soon as we got off the club grounds and were headed home he went back to his normal self.

As I grew more experienced with Harold and other horses I learned that when things were not going well with the horse it meant we had gone too far and needed to back up a step or two. Looking back on that day at the club I now do things differently. Instead of hanging onto my agenda of getting him to the club for a workout, now I would pay attention to his resistance and work from a place of finding comfort for him, enabling him to rebuild trust by knowing that I am paying attention to what he needs from me in that moment.

Lesson #7 – Lead, Follow, Get Out of the Way, or Collaborate

Chris Irwin uses the expression "lead, follow, or get out of the way" a lot when working with horses. I don't know if he coined the phrase but it is thought provoking and apt. For horses, leadership is a pragmatic requirement. For them every relationship has this element that needs to be sorted: if you are not the leader then I am and vice versa. Being able to demonstrate leadership to a horse, in the moment - every moment, is a requirement in order for that horse to know where it stands with you and feel safe with you. Trust in you as a leader can only come from the consistent demonstration of your fitness to lead. Horses can trust others in the herd that are at the same level or lower in the hierarchy. If you are consistent, then you are reliable and can be trusted. Being a follower is not necessarily a lesser role.

With people, knowing when you are not the leader is as important as knowing when you are. When we try to lead and don't have the presence, credentials, expertise, or the respect and trust of our team, then we aren't really the leader. With humans, leadership is often confused with titles and power. Understanding the difference is essential to real effectiveness in the workplace and everywhere else in life. Collaboration, delegation, and shared leadership are all possible with people where safety, respect and trust are in place. The old paradigm of the top-down corporate dictatorship doesn't work in this age of knowledge economies, nor does the notion of leadership embedded in a single person.

New models of shared leadership are springing up around the world and are an inspiration and a hope that in these troubled times we will not revert to the leader as warrior or bully. Leadership in the 21st century requires an evolutionary shift in the human species. It requires concerted sustained effort and every one of us has a responsibility to fulfill this new kind of leadership. We are all leaders in this task.

Appendix I

Triple Loop Learning

The study of learning and the human mind is an immense area of investigation. Learning how we learn and how our brains work is revolutionizing society. Learning doesn't have to change us but what a bonus when it does! Triple loop learning is an idea I came across while studying to become an executive coach. When I first encountered it I immediately recognized triple loop learning as a description of what had happened to me in my experiences with horses, as well as what was happening to my clients in our coaching sessions.

Triple loop learning is a concept about a type of learning that was initially inferred by Chris Argyris and Donald Schön (Hummelbrunner & Reynolds, 2013), and has been referenced and discussed by other thinkers and authors such as Richard Hummelbrunner and Martin Reynolds, (2013),Bateson (1973), Mark (2006), Gilmore and Warren (2007), Peschle (2007), and Jakimow (2008). There appears to be no single definition of triple loop learning, and in fact the definition of single and double loop learning are not carved in stone either. Let's back up and look at single and double loop learning first.

Simply put, single loop learning is seen as the transfer of, or the acquisition of knowledge. It is the creation of a solution to a problem where input and output are seen to be close in time and space, without too much room for questioning. It is also described as learning to adapt. One writer describes single loop learning like a thermostat that is programmed to go on or off based on its determination of the temperature. Too cold? Switch on the heat until the optimum temperature is reached, then switch off. Single loop responses recognize or create a change, and react with a prescribed response. In terms of organizational learning theory it describes the activities that result from conditions that are recognizable and require no questioning - the "this is the way we do things" approach.

Double loop learning describes learning that incorporates a feedback loop where the output of the single loop forms new input that potentially creates a change that can produce different output to the single loop. In double loop learning there is an option to ask why, to question the results, and to seek improvements. Double loop learning is nevertheless, a way of building a better mouse trap instead of building the mouse trap the way we have been doing it for years – the single loop mouse trap if you will.

Triple loop learning describes the potential to go beyond the limiting mechanisms of single and double loop learning. It is learning that is transformative. Someone described triple loop learning as being in a state of learning that is difficult to articulate. It offers the opportunity to question what is, imagine what could be, and posits an opening into creating something entirely new. In triple loop learning we question our assumptions, beliefs, and mental models, and engage in a process of discovery of what could be from an ideal perspective – not just a better version of what is. It is the land of the 'Aha' experience where invention and creativity are most at home. Triple loop learning is moving into the territory that Einstein would have us go – using a different, creative, perhaps ingenious mind to solve the problems we have created.

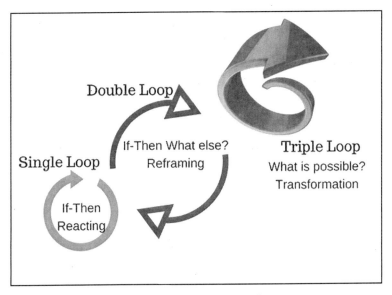

Single, Double, and Triple Loop Learning

My own personal experience and the experience of my clients while coaching with horses lies in the realm of triple loop learning. My clients experience what I call "time-release learning bombs". A common feature of this amazing work is that the learning unfolds in the moment, and then continues to play with the unconscious mind. Like the process of the Aha, it returns again and again over time, presenting new lessons and new perspectives. The memories laid down in sessions with the horses are vivid and easily recalled providing strong anchors for recall days, weeks, months and years later.

Appendix II

The Neuroscience and Physiology of Equine Facilitated Executive Coaching

"An important and well-verified law in quantum mechanics called the Quantum Zeno Effect turns out to be the key to understanding how focused attention can systematically re-wire the brain.... The Quantum Zeno Effect for neuroscience application states that the mental act of focusing attention holds in place brain circuits associated with what is being focused on. If you pay enough attention to a certain set of brain connections, it keeps this relevant circuitry stable, open and dynamically alive, enabling it to eventually becoming a part of the brain's hard wiring."
Jeffrey Schwartz, A Brain-based Approach to Coaching (Rock & Schwartz, A Brain-Based Approach to Coaching, 2006)

An explosion of research has been done in recent years on the physiology of the brain and its interactions with our bodies. The introduction of fMRI (functional Magnetic Resonance Imaging) for research across many disciplines has resulted in our learning much more about the inner workings of the brain, as well as the heart, stomach and the interaction of these major organs, which are now identified to have embodied cognition. Research is helping to explain in much greater detail the delicate interplay of chemistry and physiology between our brains and our bodies, and indeed is contributing to an explosion of medical and non-medical treatments, that heal physical, emotional, and psychological ailments and trauma.

Functional Magnetic Resonance Imaging permits us to look at the way our brains' networks of neurons fire while we are engaged in activities as well as when we are at rest or meditating. No longer are we theorizing about how our brains operate based on static pictures taken out of a context or by surgical intervention. fMRI enables us to peer into the workings of the brain while it is at work.

It turns out that Freud was right – our brains are pain-avoiding, pleasure-seeking organs. Scientists now refer to these instincts as the threat-reward response which is how our brains fundamentally categorize everything. If something is not a threat than it is a reward. There is no neutral in this categorization system. Think about that for a minute. My guess is you didn't know that your brain saw the world in such a black-and-white manner. (The threat-reward response is described by neuroscientist Evian Gordon as the "fundamental organizing principle of the brain.") (Rock, Managing with the Brain in Mind, Autumn 2009)

In addition to seeing the world in this binary, black and white way, our brains see threats faster than rewards. This is evolutionary logic - we must see threats first and we must see them faster if we are to survive. Even if we identify false positives, we increase our odds for surviving.

Not only do we see threats faster, but our physiological response – the release of adrenaline, increased heart rate, intake of oxygen and glucose utilization, – takes longer to recover from and return to normal than from perceived rewards. Research also shows us that the threats our brains perceive, such as the threat of being socially ostracized or a minor threat to our sense of status, are recognized in much the same way that we perceive the threat of a life-threatening situation or predator. (Rock & Page, Coaching With the Brain in Mind: Foundations for Practice, 2009)

Living as we do in the Westernized civilization of the

21st century, it is difficult for us to comprehend and remain cognizant of the degree to which we are still governed by the reptilian brain, the part of our neuroanatomy that governs fight, freeze, or flight, and decision-making, and is essential to our processing of emotions. We like to believe that we are rational, analytical, evolved beings but science is demonstrating there is more myth than fact. Research is calling into question our ability to rationally choose or make decisions; it appears that we have what David Rock has called "free won't" instead of free will (Shermer, 2012).

"A new study found activity in a tiny clump of 256 neurons that enabled scientists to predict with 80 percent accuracy which choice a subject would make before the person himself knew. ... Free won't is veto power over innumerable neural impulses tempting us to act in one way, such that our decision to act in another way is a real choice." (Schermer, 2012) Much or even all of what we think we are rationally analyzing is the result of chemical processes and activation of brain circuits that have taken place in our bodies and minds below the level of conscious thought, prior to our conscious mind becoming aware of them. However exerting will power over a variety of urges is an example of acting with volition and choosing what path not to take, thus earning the label "free won't".

Our brains are shaped by our relationships. Most of our brains' background processes involve thinking about ourselves and other people. From an evolutionary perspective it makes sense. We have evolved to live in families and tribal societies therefore a great deal of our brain is devoted to managing our relationships. The prolonged dependence we have upon parents and other family members for survival demands that we develop social skills to manage the complexities of interaction and the stressors associated with living in groups.

Most of the strategies and behaviours in body language and non-verbal communication that humans have developed over the millennia act below the level of our consciousness. The unspoken and often unconscious ritual behaviours that we exhibit are designed to minimize the perception of threats and maximize the reward sequences. Hand-shaking, eye contact or the avoidance of eye contact, head nodding, and the various positions we unconsciously assume in public spaces such as elevators, are examples of socially motivated behaviours that are designed to act as short-hand signaling "I am not a threat".

The Amygdala at Work

A Project Manager was hired to deliver a critical upgrade to a piece of IT infrastructure that had a direct interface with our customers. This PM was known to be able to deliver on time under adverse conditions although, as I would learn, his interpersonal skills left a little to be desired. I assigned a Support Technician from my group to attend weekly project meetings in order to keep Customer Service and Support in the loop on the schedule and impact of changes as they came up. This organization had a poor track record of keeping Support apprised of changes; oftentimes customers knew about changes before the Support team did. At one project meeting the PM turned on the Support Tech demanding to know what value he thought he was bringing to the project. The PM wanted everyone carrying his weight and contributing. The Support Tech, unused to this sort of very direct confrontational approach, promptly fainted.

Emergency Services was called. The project meeting was cancelled. Many senior leaders ended up being drawn into meetings to measure the risk to the project, to gauge potential legal liability, to understand what had happened and why, and to determine what, if anything, should be done about it. Although ultimately it was determined no physical harm had been done to the employee and no legal fallout was likely to occur, everyone involved was deeply affected. A certain amount of trust and a lot of 'face' were lost by some. A project valued at $250K suddenly had its time and cost projections threatened because an amygdalae did what it is programmed to do.

This episode was an extreme example of high emotion, and yet it is not uncommon in the workplace. It is easy to find stories of bullies and bad leaders acting out in the office. The undercurrents and influence of emotions and temperament are undeniable, and must be accommodated in order for a workplace to be considered healthy. We are emotional creatures; we cannot operate, learn or be successful in relationships without accounting for emotions, and yet they are the least likely topic to be included in discussions about performance, wellness and effectiveness in the workplace.

Speaking about emotions is useful; it reduces their impact on us, such as the amygdala response (Rock & Page, Coaching With the Brain in Mind: Foundations for Practice, 2009). If one tries to suppress emotional arousal, the limbic system stays at the same high level or gets worse. That level of arousal diminishes cognitive function, reduces field of vision, the capacity of working memory, significantly reduces insight, creates more threat responses, limits input about what other people are saying, and negatively impacts the ability to process information. In addition, suppressing emotions makes blood pressure spike and will likely make other people emotionally uncomfortable (affect contagion), even though they may be unaware of the reaction they are having, or why (Rock, Managing with the Brain in Mind, Autumn 2009).

How Many Brains Do We Have?

We now understand that humans have several brains, the oldest being the reptilian brain which monitors and manages autonomic functions and the sympathetic and parasympathetic systems. The reptilian brain governs our instinctive reactions to threats and rewards. The threat response is faster and lasts longer than the reward response.

In addition to the reptilian brain, we have at least three other brains: the paleo-mammalian brain or limbic system, the neocortex, and the brain in our gut. The Heart Math Institute posits that we have a brain in our heart as well. "Over the past several decades, several lines of scientific evidence have established that, far more than a mechanical pump, the heart functions as a sensory organ and as a complex information encoding and processing center." (Rollin Mccraty, Atkinson, Tomasino, & Bradley, 2009) These other brains are integral to the processing and regulating of instincts, emotions, our ability to learn and remember, as well as our abstract thinking and language abilities.

The brain in our stomach is likely the least understood by science, but research now shows that a significant number of neurons send information from the gut to the brain, indicating that it operates with some independence but it is not simply a relay station for the cerebral functions. (Pasricha M.D., 2011) The 'gut feeling' we talk about is in fact the result of some sort of chemical conversation between our stomachs and our brains. (Hadhazy, 2010)

David Rock has introduced some significant neuroscience concepts into the domain of organizational behaviour. He founded the Neuroleadership Institute to bring scientists and non-scientists together to pursue research through scientific methods and analyse results with the goal of applying brain-based science to improve the effectiveness of leadership training and development.

One example is his model known as SCARF, the acronym for Status, Certainty, Autonomy, Relatedness, and Fairness, which articulates the brain's primary areas of interest in how we relate to ourselves and each other. Given our propensity to see change as threatening due to the always-on-duty amygdala, Rock's model may enable leaders to minimize, or at least positively influence, the negative perceptions of change in the workplace by planning mitigations for the greatest known areas of threat.

Getting Emotions onto the Risk Register

I was responsible for an IT department that was subject to a number of reorganizations over several years. Given that I was the change agent in most of these reorganizations, the degree of stress that impacted me had more to do with work load than with any of the SCARF domains. For most of these changes I was unaware of the neuroscience at play and the importance of the SCARF model for myself and my staff. The last big reorganization that I led involved moving me from a role as a line manager to more of a project manager role; my first mission was to reorganize and consolidate two different groups into a new, larger, more effective department. One of the staff reporting to me suffered fairly extreme stress during this reorganization, and although I could see it happening, I was unable to understand how to mitigate the stress and create a positive effect with this person and our relationship deteriorated considerably resulting in her voluntary departure.

Around the time of this person's departure I came across

David Rock's article on the SCARF model, and realized the ways in which this person had been adversely affected in all dimensions according to the model. In this reorganization she had lost status, certainty, autonomy, relatedness, and perceived it all to be unfair. I regretted not being able to help her. She was a talented resource who was a loss to the department. Too late I realized how we can mitigate the risks associated with change and reorganization if we are careful to notice and anticipate the impacts on people.

Being more self-aware of the architecture of our brains can help to make us more empathic and caring, and helps us to understand our own experience, create more choice in our lives and in the lives of others. Rock contends, and I agree, that leaders could have a more positive impact in these situations by being aware of these neurological dimensions and compensate for them when they are not being met. Where status and certainty are affected, meeting the needs of autonomy, relatedness or fairness can compensate. Organizations would do well to incorporate these concepts into change planning.

Why Does This Matter?

Coaching with horses generates the ideal conditions for insight, transformational learning, an opening creative mind, and lateral thinking. The experience of having our brains and bodies engaged in mindful activities with a 1200 pound sentient beast moves us to a place where we are able to change our perceptions. The act of spending time with them in mindful awareness, in what Jeffrey Schwartz calls the quantum zeno state of attention density, generates experiences that can and do re-wire the brain. A brain rewired is a brain that is changed. And this is a good thing.

Appendix III

The 8 Fold Path of Equus

My friend and horse trainer Chris Irwin developed a beautiful model that he uses in his coaching that he has called the 8 Fold Path of Equus, with acknowledgements to the Buddha. The Buddhist 8 Fold Path is a guide to living and practicing an honourable life that is considered to be the heart of Buddhist practice. The steps, which are not linear, include right view, right intention, right action, right speech, right livelihood, right effort, right mindfulness, and right concentration. When one follows these steps then one can expect to live a spiritual life that may lead to enlightenment.

The 8 Fold Path of Equus is modeled to reflect the work of riding and being with the horse. Thus each of these non-linear steps reflects ways of being that promote harmony between the horse and human. They serve as an excellent model for a coaching engagement as they can identify areas in life where we may need to prioritize our attention.

I carefully modeled Chris' 8 steps and aligned them with emotional intelligence and the phases that one might examine to achieve greater effectiveness and actualization in one's life.

The steps are as follows:

Alignment: "Position yourself strategically" is a fundamental leadership and safety principle when working with horses. Horses are highly aware of our physical limitations relative to them so in order to leverage our strengths we must be highly aware of how we position ourselves in relation to them. This same precept applies in relation to all the elements in your life. In order to live a life that has meaning and value we must do some self-analysis. When we are on our path, alignment is important to ensure we are able to move toward our goals with clarity. Are the people and organizations you are connected to aligned with your goals and values? Do you have a vision for your life? Do you know yourself and what will create the life you want for yourself and loved ones? From an EQ perspective, alignment relates to self-regard and problem solving.

Forward: How are you moving through life? For an equestrian, forward is about impulsion in the horse. For humans forward is about the ability to hold one's ideal future in focus and maintain the ability to channel one's energies to move through life while letting go of counter-productive behaviours. Forward is also about knowing your purpose. Do you have a mission and understand your purpose? From an EQ perspective, Forward relates to assertiveness.

Contact: When working with horses, either in the saddle or on the ground, contact is an important characteristic of communication and defines the relationship. Contact is the way a rider communicates with the horse through the reins, seat, and legs. Riders want their horses to seek contact which means that the horse is comfortable with the rider's seat, hands and legs, is trusting, and is willing to move under the rider's direction. How are you at communicating? How are you in relationship to yourself, others, and the universe? How are you at engendering trust and connection? From an EQ perspective, contact is about interpersonal relationships and empathy.

Timing: When it comes to timing Kenny Rogers said it best: "You've got to know when to hold 'em, know when to fold 'em, know when to walk away and know when to run". With horses timing is key. The right timing of a request to move from a trot to a canter will result in a horse moving in a state of relaxation or experiencing frustration or agitated by interference. Timing is knowing when to execute on a decision that has been planned in the seconds or weeks before implementation. How are you at maintaining awareness of your emotional state and decision-making on a moment-to-moment and day-to-day basis? Are you coping with life? Is it time to stop coping and make changes? Or is the time not quite right to introduce the stresses and strains that come from change? Timing is about dealing with that which is not serving you and knowing when to act. From an EQ perspective, timing is about emotional self-awareness, problem-solving, and decision-making. Recognizing the best time to act - or not - comes from this skillset.

Calm: Horses are mammals like us and like us they seek calm and relaxation. Stress in a horse is very much like stress in humans; stress is impossible to avoid completely but it can interfere with learning and have a detrimental effect on health. When we are calm we are living spiritually, physically, and emotionally in tune in a state of well being - in a state of equanimity. Calm is an expression of our ability to feel passion and excitement while maintaining composure. From an EQ perspective, calm is about stress management and impulse control.

Bend: In the horse, bend, at its most simple, occurs when a horse yields her barrel or ribcage away from the leg of her rider on request. This ability is a desirable skill that assists a rider to develop the athleticism and balance a horse requires to carry a rider. Balance in all aspects of our lives is described by bend. Life doesn't go according to our plans. How are you at accepting what is, letting go of that which you cannot control or change, and moving forward towards achieving your goals. From an EQ perspective, bend is about flexibility.

Boundaries: The horse is a master at discovering our gaps. These are typically called evasions in the horse and occur when a horse reads us, identifies the areas that we are not paying attention to, and exploits the gap to achieve its own ends. Horses usually respond well to clear consistent boundaries and much of the skill of horsemanship is learning and responding to the horse's demand for clear consistent boundaries. Leadership of self and others is how boundaries show up in our lives. Knowing our values enable us to change course as required. Feeling secure enough in ourselves to seek input from trusted others is an important part of success. From an EQ perspective, boundaries is about reality-testing.

Collection: When a horse is collected it has shifted its weight onto its hind legs and lifted its back. This enables the horse to become like a loaded spring, able to maneuvre and respond athletically to the requests of the rider. How do you collect, focus, and expend your energy in order to maintain an unlimited supply that is available to meet your goals. Collection is the keystone of the other seven steps in the 8 Fold Path of Equus. From an EQ perspective, collection is about self-actualization; self-actualization enables the manifestation of our ideal life.

You may take the confidential complimentary self-test at www.equinecoach.ca. You will receive your individualized results within minutes. If you don't receive them please check the spam folder in your email set-up. You are likely to find your report there. However if you don't find it there please contact me so I can generate a copy for you.

Epilogue

I am a sceptic and a bit of an intellectual. One of the reasons I am so enamoured with horses and coaching is because it has been such a powerfully positive and spiritually unifying force in my life. I tend to live in my pre-frontal cortex and having worked most of my career in the knowledge sector, I get positive reinforcement for it. So being with horses is highly therapeutic and from my perspective, much more fun than sitting on a cushion in zazen. Nevertheless, in mid-career I was finding my skeptical self a little tyrannical at times. When making big tough life decisions, I was missing a connection to an inner knowing, a connection that we describe as intuition. I really wanted to connect to my inner 'flake' (as my outer sceptic would like to call her).

To be honest, I had experienced many strange and still unexplained occurrences in my youth and early twenties that I found disturbing and scary. I didn't like them and managed to shut down that intuitive side of myself so that I could get on with the practicalities of life. By the mid-nineties, I had come to a place in life though where I really wanted to reconnect with whatever that mysterious part of being human is. While I do call myself a sceptic I am in fact a believer in the power of unseen forces, be they gamma rays, EMF, or other as-yet-to-be-measured energies. That said, when people tell me that animals speak to them I accept this in the same way that I accept people saying God has spoken to them. I consider that kind of communication personal and not prescriptive.

From that first life-changing riding lesson in 1998, I knew I was going to find that connection through the time I would spend with horses. (I certainly wasn't going to find it at work in IT.) I had already begun to manifest things in my life that seemed impossible, a couple of cars that were given to me when I most needed transportation and couldn't afford it, a couple of wonderful career-making jobs, and sums of money that came from nowhere. Once I started to experience being in touch with my intuition again I began to envision greater things in my life, things that fulfilled life-long passions, such as getting to know horses.

Despite not knowing how I would put together a career with horses and helping people (that didn't involve becoming a therapist), I began to focus on it and started to really connect to the feeling of following my heart. I began to envision having the seemingly impossible in my life – my own horse among other things.

Within only a couple of years of envisioning having my own horse, Easter's Hurricane, barn name 'Harold', became my horse. Much like the way I felt when I first became a mother, I felt incompetent and scared of the enormous responsibility but I knew it was right for both he and I. Having the responsibility for the well-being of such an enormous and somewhat mysterious animal was sobering but I soon adjusted and over the years I learned a lot about horses that I would have otherwise never have learned. He became my first co-coach and together we explored and developed a methodology of how to do equine facilitated executive coaching.

We had one of those once-in-a-lifetime horse-human relationships. He was my horse and I was his person. Everyone remarked on the fact that when I was around he was a different animal. When we first met he was shut down like an autistic child. He had not bonded with anyone for as long as most people knew him but somehow he bonded with me and I, of course, with him. He was a middle-aged horse when we met and he became a senior under my care. Having been at the track for many years he came with the injuries and illnesses that go along with the hard life of a well-used thoroughbred. I had the pleasure of seeing him retire and become a real horse in his old age, spending time in a field mowing the lawn and playing with another horse at liberty.

The time came, after 11 years together, to send my beloved horse to whatever lies beyond. He was nearing his 28th birthday and the damage done from his early years at the track was taking its toll. It had become our habitual greeting in the last years that, as he saw me coming down the path, he would lower his head, walk from his paddock into his stall, and be hanging his head over the stall door as I arrived. I would then open the door and stand back to let him out. He would step out and go immediately down the shedrow and around the corner to say hello to his friend Donovan in the back paddock. Then he would meander back to the patch of grass at the edge of the fenced-off field and mow the grass. (It should be noted that this desire to say hello to his friend may not have been pure altruism at work; I sometimes thought it was his way of making sure that his friend knew he was out eating grass while Donovan had to stay behind and make do with his hay.)

When it started to happen that I opened his stall door and he didn't step out, I knew he was physically hurting. The question was 'how much'. Like pre-verbal babies, animals can't tell us in words how and where it hurts. With horses, there is the added complication that, as prey animals, they are reluctant to show illness or injury lest the predators single them out. With a horse, by the time it is apparent that there is pain, the injury or illness is significant and they can't hide it anymore. In addition to the injuries and impairments that create problems for horses, they pose a risk that other pets do not; ill horses become a potential risk to themselves and their handlers if they go down and can't get up or go down without warning, especially in an enclosed space such as a stall.

Eventually I made one of the hardest decisions in my life. After consulting with my veterinarian and many experienced equestrians, I decided to euthanize him before his condition became dangerous to himself and people. As I started to tell my close friends and confess that I wasn't sure I could manage to be there for him, I had many offers of help.

People wanted to be there for me and him; they knew how hard it was going to be. My beloved horse was teaching me yet another major life lesson. For me, asking for help has always been extremely difficult, often impossible. My mother used to say that the first words I spoke were "I do it myself". I have always had great difficulty asking for help or relying on others to help me in my personal life. But knowing how much love was being offered to both of us, I allowed these dear friends to help me in my vulnerability. It is a decision I have never regretted.

When the time came, there were eight of us standing with him including the vet. The day had dawned with ugly March stormy clouds and slashing rain but as the time drew near the sun burst through the clouds and bathed us all in the hopeful renewal of a glorious spring day. We walked him out into the field and the vet administered the drugs that would render him unconscious and then stop his heart. As the drugs started to work in his body I noticed a single tear run from his left eye. He nodded his head once to me, turned slightly to nod to his trainer Lyz, and then a little more to nod once to his friend Naoko. Once he was gone and I had said my last goodbyes, I returned alone to his stall while the others waited for the truck that would take him away for a necropsy and cremation.

As I bent over to return the hoof pick and curry comb to

his grooming kit, I suddenly felt the temperature plummet to near freezing. The sky, minutes ago a brilliant early spring blue, was now ominously brutishly black. A violent wind came from somewhere behind me and as I stood up, like a banshee, it swooped down the shedrow between the barn and the high hedge. Ignoring the first three stalls, the wind unhooked the upper stall door in front of me and furiously slammed it shut with a bang. Just as suddenly as it arose, the wind was gone; unearthly quiet settled in and the temperature returned to normal.

Resources

"A Brief Introduction to the Default Mode Network." YouTube, 2011. Web. 13 Aug. 2016.

Buckner, R. L., J. R. Andrews-Hanna, and D. L. Schacter. "The Brain's Default Network: Anatomy, Function, and Relevance to Disease." *Annals of the New York Academy of Sciences* 1124.1 (2008): 1-38. Web. Retrieved from www.psych.colorado. edu/~hannaje/Publications_&_CV_files/Buckner_et_al_ANYAS_2008.pdf

Chamberlin, J. Edward. Horse: *How the Horse Has Shaped Civilizations*. New York: BlueBridge, 2006. Print.

Chamorro-Premuzic, T. (2013). Why Do So Many Incompetent Men Become Leaders? Retrieved August 11, 2016, from www.hbr.org/2013/08/why-do-so-many-incompetent-men

Ekman, Paul. Paul Ekman Group. Retrieved from www.paulekman.com/micro-expressions/

Flood, Robert L., and Norma R. A. Romm. *Diversity Management: Triple Loop Learning*. Chichester: J. Wiley, 1996. Print.

Gallo, Carmine. Talk Like TED: The 9 *Public Speaking Secrets of the World's Top Minds*. 125. St. Martin's, 2014. Print.

Gill, Stephen J. *Developing a Learning Culture in Nonprofit Organizations*. Los Angeles: SAGE, 2010. Print. Appendix

Goleman, D. (2007). *Social intelligence: The Revolutionary New Science of Human Relationships*. New York: Bantam Books.

Gonzales, Laurence. *Everyday Survival: Why Smart People Do Stupid Things*. New York: W.W. Norton, 2008. Print.

Howard, Pierce J. *The Owner's Manual for the Brain: Everyday Applications from Mind-brain Research*. Bard, 2006. Print.

Hummelbrunner , Richard and Reynolds, Martin (2013). Systems thinking, learning and values in evaluation. Evaluation Connections (EES Newsletter)

Irwin, Chris, and Bob Weber. *Dancing with Your Dark Horse: How Horse Sense Helps Us Find Balance, Strength, and Wisdom*. New York: Marlowe, 2005. Print.

Irwin, Chris, and Bob Weber. *Horses Don't Lie: What Horses Teach Us about Our Natural Capacity for Awareness, Confidence, Courage, and Trust*. New York: Marlowe, 2001. Print.

Klinger E. (1971). *Structure and Functions of Fantasy*. 347. New York: Wiley

Martin, J. (17 January 2014). For Senior Leaders, Fit Matters More than Skill. Retrieved August 11, 2016, from www.hbr.org/2014/01/for-senior-leaders-fit-matters-more-than-skill

Mayer, John D., Peter Salovey, and David R. Caruso. "Emotional Intelligence: Theory, Findings, and Implications." *Psychological Inquiry* 15.3 (2004): 197-215. Web. 11 June 2016.

McAdams, Dan P. "The Mind of Donald Trump." *The Atlantic*. Atlantic Media Company, June 2016. Web. 11 June 2016. Retrieved from www.theatlantic.com/magazine/archive/2016/06/the-mind-of-donald-trump/480771/

Mccraty, Rollin, Ph.D., Mike Atkinson, Dana Tomasino, B.A., and William A. Tiller, Ph.D. "The Electricity of Touch: Detection and Measurement of Cardiac Energy Exchange Between People-Page 1 - *HeartMath Institute*." HeartMath Institute. N.p., n.d. Web.

Rock, David, and Jeffrey M. Schwartz, M.C. "A Brain-Based Approach to Coaching." *International Journal of Coaching in Organizations* 4 (2006): 32-43. Web. 23 May 2016.

Mccraty, Rollin, Ph.D. "Science of the Heart - *HeartMath Institute*." HeartMath Institute. HeartMath Institute, Nov. 2015. Web. 09 May 2016. Vol. 2

Mccraty, Rollin, Ph.D., Mike Atkinson, Dana Tomasino, B.A., and Raymond Trevor Bradley, Ph.D. "The Coherent Heart: Heart Brain Interactions, Psychophysiological Coherence, and the Emergence of System-Wide Order." *Internal Review* 5.2 (2009): 50. Web.

Ovans, Andrea. "How Emotional Intelligence Became a Key Leadership Skill." *Harvard Business Review*. N.p., 28 Apr. 2015. Web. 13 Aug. 2016. Retrieved from www.hbr.org/2015/04/how-emotional-intelligence-became-a-key-leadership-skill

Pasricha, Pankaj, M.D. "Stanford Hospital's Pankaj Pasricha Discusses the Enteric Nervous System, or Brain in Your Gut." *Enteric Nervous System.* Stanford Health Care, 03 Feb. 2011. Web. 12 Aug. 2016.

Pentland, Alex Sandy The New Science of Building Great Teams. *Harvard Business Review* (April 2012): Web. 31 May 2016.

Peschle, M.F. "Triple Loop Learning as Foundation for Profound Change, Individual Cultivation, and Radical Innovation." Constructivist Foundations 2 (2007): 136-45. Web

Porges, Stephen W. "The Polyvagal Perspective." *Biological Psychology* 74.2 (2007): 116-43. Web. www.ncbi.nlm.nih.gov/ pmc/articles/PMC1868418/?report=reader May 10, 2016

Rock, David, and Jeffrey M. Schwartz, M.D. "A Brain-based Approach to Coaching." *International Journal of Coaching in Organizations* (2006): 32-43. Web.

Rock, David, and Linda J. Page. *Coaching with the Brain in Mind: Foundations for Practice.* Hoboken, NJ: Wiley, 2009. Print.

Rock, David. *"Managing with the Brain in Mind."* Strategy Business. 352-53., Autumn 2009. Web. 12

Rock, David. "David Rock: The AHA Moment." www.davidrock.net/files/TheAhaMomentASTD2011.pdf 2011 Web 27 Apr. 2016

Romme, A. Georges L., and Arjen Van Witteloostuijn. "Circular Organizing and Triple Loop Learning." *Journal of OrgChange Mgmt Journal of Organizational Change Management* 12.5 (1999): 439-54. Web.

Siegel, Dan. "*Wheel of Awareness*." Dr. Dan Siegel. N.p., n.d. Web. 27 Apr. 2016. Retrieved from www.drdansiegel.com/resources/wheel_of_awareness/

Sonnenburg, Justin, and Erica Sonnenburg. "Gut Feelings–the "Second Brain" in Our Gastrointestinal Systems [Excerpt]." *Scientific American*. N.p., 1 May 2015. Web.

Trungpa, Chogyam. *The Collected Works of Chogyam Trungpa*. Vol. III. Boston, MA: Shambhala, 2004. 219. Google Books. Shambala Publications. Web.

"The Heart-Brain Connection - *HeartMath Institute*." HeartMath Institute. N.p., n.d. Web. 13 Aug. 2016.

Williams, W. (2015, October 1). The Secret Lives of Horses. Retrieved from www.scientificamerican.com/article/the-secret-lives-of-horses/

Willis, Judy. ""What You Should Know about Your Brain," by Judy Willis " Educational Leadership, 2009. Web. 12 Aug. 2016. www.scientificamerican.com/article/gut-second-brain/

Willis, Judy, M.D. "The Neuroscience Behind Stress and Learning." www.edutopia.org/. N.p., 18 July 2014. Web. 13 Aug. 2016.

Author Biography

Equine Coach Founder, Evelyn McKelvie is a certified credentialed Executive Coach who coaches people with the assistance of horses. A pioneer in the equine facilitated coaching movement, her own unique approach respects the true nature of the horse as well as her clients.

Evelyn's career path has been very much "a road less travelled". Over the years Evelyn explored the fields of art, music, theatre, and has held leadership roles in post-secondary education, and Information Technology. In 2014 she retired from the University of British Columbia's IT Enterprise Architecture group to coach full time. Evelyn's clients benefit from the many years of coaching and horse training and the wealth of real-world experience she brings to her coaching.

As a certified horse trainer and Executive Coach, Evelyn incorporates techniques from the worlds of neuroscience and Emotional Intelligence into her work. You can find out more, or take the complimentary self-test - The 8 Fold Path of Equus, at www.equinecoach.ca.

Contact: info@equinecoach.ca

About Evelyn

Evelyn currently works in a couple of locations in the Vancouver, B.C. area and is able to travel to deliver workshops or retreats. She offers a number of coaching programs for individuals and designs custom retreats and off-site experiences for groups and teams. Evelyn is certified to deliver EQ-I (emotional intelligence) assessments for individuals and teams. These reports provide clients with a wealth of information and self-knowledge that enhance the coaching journey.

Viam Equus (The Knight's Path) is a program of workshops offered for open registration. These workshops include:

- The Power of Awareness and Presence,
- The Power of Conscious Communication, and
- The Power of Mindful Leadership

Evelyn works in collaboration with other coaches to produce workshops that focus on topics such as assertiveness and presentation skills.

The Executive Horse is available for sale on Amazon as well as on Evelyn's website:
www.equinecoach.ca

Contact Evelyn at info@equinecoach.ca to inquire about working with her or designing a custom program for yourself or your team.